# EMPIRICISM AND THE PHILOSOPHY OF MIND

# Empiricism and the Philosophy of Mind

WILFRID SELLARS

*With an Introduction by* RICHARD RORTY
*and a Study Guide by* ROBERT BRANDOM

Harvard University Press
Cambridge, Massachusetts
London, England

*Empiricism and the Philosophy of Mind* was originally published in *Minnesota
Studies in the Philosophy of Science*, vol. 1., ed. Herbert Feigl and Michael
Scriven (Minneapolis: University of Minnesota Press, 1956).

**Library of Congress Cataloging-in-Publication Data**

Sellars, Wilfrid.
    Empiricism and the philosophy of mind / Wilfrid Sellars ; with an
introduction by Richard Rorty, and a study guide by Robert Brandom.
        p.    cm.
    Taken from Minnesota studies in the philosophy of science, v. 1,
The Foundations of science and the concepts of psychology and
psychoanalysis.
    Includes bibliographical references.
    ISBN 0-674-25154-7 (cloth : alk. paper)
    ISBN 0-674-25155-5 (pbk. : alk. paper)
    1. Philosophy of mind. 2. Empiricism — Controversial literature.
3. Analysis (Philosophy). 4. Sellars, Wilfrid. Empiricism and the
philosophy of mind. I. Rorty, Richard. II. Brandom, Robert.
III. Title.
BD418.3.S45    1997
128'.2 — dc21
96-51811

# Contents

# EMPIRICISM AND THE PHILOSOPHY OF MIND

RICHARD RORTY

THE KIND OF PHILOSOPHY we now call "analytic" started out as a form of empiricism. It developed out of the work of Bertrand Russell, Rudolf Carnap, and others—the work summarized and put in canonical, easily teachable, form by A. J. Ayer in his *Language, Truth, and Logic* (1936). In that book, Ayer put forward the ideas which make up what we now call "logical positivism" or "logical empiricism"— ideas which restated the foundationalist epistemology of British empiricism in linguistic, as opposed to psychological, terms. These ideas are very different from those which underlie what is sometimes called "post-positivistic" analytic philosophy—a brand of philosophy which is sometimes said to be "beyond" empiricism and rationalism.

The shift from the earlier to the later form of analytic philosophy, a shift which began around 1950 and was complete by around 1970, was a result of many complexly interacting forces, the pattern of which is hard to trace. Nevertheless, any historian of this shift would do well to focus on three seminal works: Willard van Orman Quine's "Two Dogmas of Empiricism" (1951), Ludwig Wittgenstein's *Philosophical Investigations* (1954), and Wilfrid Sellars's "Empiricism and the Philosophy of Mind" (1956).

Of these three, Sellars's long, complicated, and very rich essay is the least known and discussed. Historians of recent Anglo-American philosophy have emphasized the importance of Quine's essay in raising doubts about the notion of "analytic truth" and thus about the Carnapian-Russellian notion that philosophy should be "the logical analysis of language." They have also emphasized the importance of the work of the later Wittgenstein—especially what Strawson called his "hostility to immediacy," his distrust of traditional empiricist explanations of the acquisition of knowledge. They have not, for the most part, given much weight to Sellars's role in bringing about the collapse of sense-data empiricism. This is a pity, since Sellars's attack on "the Myth of the Given" was, in America (though not in Britain), very influential in persuading philosophers that there was something deeply wrong with the sort of phenomenalism Ayer had advocated.[1]

Wilfrid Sellars was born in 1912 and died in 1989. He taught philosophy at Minnesota, Yale, and finally at Pittsburgh. He published a great many essays, as well as one monograph, *Science and Metaphysics* (his Locke Lectures at Oxford in 1967).[2] His work was often criticized for its

1. Austin's criticism of Ayer in his posthumous *Sense and Sensibilia* played the role in Britain which Sellars's article played in America. Though they greatly admired Austin, American philosophers had already pretty much given up on sense-data by the time *Sense and Sensibilia* appeared.

2. *Science and Metaphysics* (London: Routledge, 1967). The most important collections of Sellars's essays are his *Science, Perception and Reality* (London: Routledge, 1963)—which contains "Empiricism and the Philosophy of Mind"—and his *Essays in Philosophy and Its History* (Dordrecht: Reidel, 1974). Commentary on Sellars's work may be found in C. F. Delaney et al., *The Synoptic Vision: Essays on the Philosophy of*

obscurity. This obscurity was partially a result of Sellars's idiosyncratic style, but some of it was in the eye of the beholder. For Sellars was unusual among prominent American philosophers of the post–World War II period, and quite different from Quine and Wittgenstein, in having a wide and deep acquaintance with the history of philosophy.[3] This knowledge of previous philosophers kept intruding into his work (as in the two rather cryptic chapters on Kant which open *Science and Metaphysics*), and helped to make his writings seem difficult for analytic philosophers whose education had been less historically oriented than Sellars's. Sellars believed that "philosophy without the history of philosophy is, if not blind, at least dumb," but this view seemed merely perverse to much of his audience.

OF ALL SELLARS'S WRITINGS, "Empiricism and the Philosophy of Mind" is the most widely read and the most accessible. Indeed, this essay is all that most analytic philosophers know of Sellars. But it is almost enough, since it is the epitome of an entire philosophical system. It covers most of the aspects of Sellars's overall project—the project he described as an attempt to usher analytic philosophy out of its Humean and into its Kantian stage.

The fundamental thought which runs through this essay is Kant's: "intuitions without concepts are blind." Having

*Wilfrid Sellars* (Notre Dame: Notre Dame University Press, 1977), and in Hector-Neri Casteneda, ed., *Action, Knowledge, and Reality: Studies in Honor of Wilfrid Sellars* (Indianapolis: Bobbs-Merrill, 1975).

3. For Quine's dismissive attitude toward the history of philosophy, see his autobiography, *The Time of My Life* (Cambridge, Mass.: MIT Press, 1985), p. 194. For Wittgenstein's spotty reading in ancient and modern philosophy, see Garth Hallett, S.J., *A Companion to Wittgenstein's 'Philosophical Investigations'* (Ithaca: Cornell University Press, 1977), pp. 759–775.

a sense-impression is, by itself, an example neither of knowledge nor of conscious experience. Sellars, like the later Wittgenstein but unlike Kant, identified the possession of a concept with the mastery of the use of a word. So for him, mastery of a language is prerequisite of conscious experience. As he says in sect. 29: "*all* awareness of *sorts, resemblances, facts*, etc., in short all awareness of abstract entities—indeed, all awareness even of particulars—is a linguistic affair." This doctrine, which he called "psychological nominalism," entails that Locke, Berkeley, and Hume were wrong in thinking that we are "aware of certain determinate sorts . . . simply by virtue of having sensations and images" (sect. 28).

Sellars's argument for psychological nominalism is based on a claim which spells out the moral of many of the aphorisms of *Philosophical Investigations:* "The essential point is that in characterizing an episode or a state as that of *knowing*, we are not giving an empirical description of that episode or state; we are placing it in the logical space of reasons, of justifying and being able to justify what one says" (sect. 36). In other words, knowledge is inseparable from a social practice—the practice of justifying one's assertions to one's fellow-humans. It is not presupposed by this practice, but comes into being along with it.

So we cannot do what some logical positivists hoped to do: analyze epistemic facts without remainder "into nonepistemic facts, whether phenomenal or behavioral, public or private, with no matter how lavish a sprinkling of subjunctives and hypotheticals" (sect. 5).[4] In particular, we can-

4. This reference to various attempted reductive analyses presupposes, as do many other passages in the essay, some familiarity with the literature of analytic philosophy in the 1940s and early 1950s—e.g., with Ayer's defenses of phenomenal-

not perform such an analysis by discovering the "foundation" of empirical knowledge in the objects of "direct acquaintance," objects which are "immediately before the mind." We cannot privilege reports that, for example, there is something red in the neighborhood as "reports of the immediately given." For such reports are no less mediated by language, and thus by social practice, than reports that there are cows or electrons in the neighborhood. The whole idea of "foundations" of knowledge, basic to both empiricism and rationalism, disappears once we become psychological nominalists.

Whereas Quine's "Two Dogmas" had helped destroy the rationalist form of foundationalism by attacking the distinction between analytic and synthetic truths, "Empiricism and the Philosophy of Mind" helped destroy the empiricist form of foundationalism by attacking the distinction between what is "given to the mind" and what is "added by the mind." Sellars's attack on the Myth of the Given was a decisive move in turning analytic philosophy away from the foundationalist motives of the logical empiricists. It raised doubts about the very idea of "epistemology," about the reality of the problems which philosophers had discussed under that heading.[5] One of the most quoted sentences in the essay occurs in sect. 38: ". . . empirical knowledge, like its sophisticated exten-

ism, Ryle's criticisms of Descartes, and so on. Certain sections of Sellars's essay — e.g., sections 8–9 and 21–23 — may seem pointless excursus to those who lack such familiarity. But the overall argument of the essay is intelligible without reference to the particular figures whom Sellars discusses.

5. Sellars's work along these lines links up with that of the American pragmatists — notably Peirce's polemics against givenness in his essay "Consequences of Four Incapacities" (1868) and Dewey's in "An Empirical Survey of Empiricisms" (1935). For a good account of the development of American pragmatism — an account from which Sellars is largely absent, but into which he fits nicely — see

sion, science, is rational, not because it has a *foundation* but
because it is a self-correcting enterprise which can put *any*
claim in jeopardy, though not *all* at once."[6] This sentence
suggests that rationality is a matter not of obedience to
standards (which epistemologists might hope to codify), but
rather of give-and-take participation in a cooperative social
project.

AN ELABORATION AND DEFENSE of the presuppositions and
implications of psychological nominalism, however, is not all
there is to "Empiricism and the Philosophy of Mind." Sections 48–63 contain Sellars's "Myth of Jones"—a story which
explains why we can be naturalists without being behaviorists, why we can accept Wittgenstein's doubts about what
Sellars calls "self-authenticating non-verbal episodes" without sharing Ryle's doubts about the existence of such mental
entities as thoughts and sense-impressions.

At the time at which Sellars was writing, this was a vexed
issue. For the appearance of Ryle's *The Concept of Mind* (1949)
shortly before that of the *Philosophical Investigations* (1954) had
made Wittgensteinian opposition to the idea of "a private
language," and to that of "entities capable of being known
by only one person," seem inseparable from Ryle's polemic
against "the ghost in the machine." Sellars's account of inner
episodes as having originally been postulated, rather than

John P. Murphy, *Pragmatism: From Peirce to Davidson* (Boulder, Colo.: Westview Press, 1990).
   6. I have offered a brief account of the roles of Quine and Sellars in persuading philosophers to abandon the atomism and foundationalism of Russell and Carnap in sect. 2 of Chapter IV of my *Philosophy and the Mirror of Nature* (1979).
   In that book I also urged that giving up foundationalism might cause us to abandon the idea that we needed a "theory of knowledge." Recently Michael

observed, entities, together with his account of how speakers might then come to make introspective reports (sect. 59) of such episodes, made clear how one could be Wittgensteinian without being Rylean. Sellars showed how one could give a non-reductive account of "mental event" while nevertheless eschewing, with Wittgenstein, the picture of the eye of the mind witnessing these events in a sort of immaterial inner theater.

Sellars's treatment of the distinction between mind and body has been followed up by many philosophers of mind in subsequent decades. He may have been the first philosopher to insist that we see "mind" as a sort of hypostatization of language. He argued that the intentionality of beliefs is a reflection of the intentionality of sentences, rather than conversely.[7] This reversal makes it possible to understand mind as gradually entering the universe by and through the gradual development of language, as part of a naturalistically explicable evolutionary process, rather than seeing language as the outward manifestation of something inward and mysterious which humans have and animals lack. As Sellars sees it, if you can explain how the social practices we call "using language" came into existence, you have already explained

Williams—in his *Unnatural Doubts: Epistemological Realism and the Basis of Scepticism* (Cambridge, Mass., and Oxford: Blackwell, 1991)—has developed this theme much more thoroughly and carefully. He argues that it is the unfortunate idea that there is a natural kind called "human knowledge" which gives rise to both foundationalism and Cartesian skepticism. Williams's earlier book—*Groundless Belief* (Blackwell, 1977)—an anti-foundationalist treatise which laid the foundations for *Unnatural Doubts*, was heavily influenced by Sellars.

7. This insistence is most explicit in Sellars's very instructive debate with Roderick Chisholm, reprinted as "Intentionality and the Mental" in *Minnesota Studies in the Philosophy of Science*, vol. 2 (Minneapolis: University of Minnesota Press, 1958).

all that needs to be explained about the relation between
mind and world.[8]

A RECENT BOOK by Robert Brandom, *Making It Explicit*,[9]
offers the first systematic and comprehensive attempt to
follow up on Sellars's thought.[10] More specifically, it offers a
"semantic explanatory strategy which takes *inference* as its
basic concept," as opposed to the alternative strategy "domi-
nant since the Enlightenment, which takes *representation* as
its basic concept."[11] Brandom's work can usefully be seen as
an attempt to usher analytic philosophy from its Kantian to

8. This is only true, however, if, like Daniel Dennett and unlike Thomas Nagel,
one does not think of "what it is like to see something red" as referring to something
quite different than does "having the disposition to call something red." To agree
that Sellars dissolved the mind-body problem, one has to deny the existence of
qualia. It is not clear that Sellars would be on Dennett's side of this issue, however,
since he was tempted to think that what he called "the scientific image of man"
would be incomplete until we discover special new microstructural properties
capable of accounting for "the ultimate homogeneity" of phenomenological presen-
tations. Be that as it may, Dennett has made clear his own indebtedness to Sellars.
See his *The Intentional Stance* (Cambridge, Mass.: Bradford Books, 1986). At p. 341
Dennett gives Sellars credit for originating functionalism, the school of thought in
contemporary philosophy of mind to which Dennett himself belongs. In a footnote
on that page, Dennett remarks that "Sellars's influence has been ubiquitous but
almost subliminal," and at p. 349 he says, "Almost no one cites Sellars, while
reinventing his wheels with gratifying regularity." This latter remark seems to me
an accurate account of Sellars's role in recent analytic philosophy.
    9. *Making It Explicit: Reasoning, Representing, and Discursive Commitment* (Cambridge,
Mass.: Harvard University Press, 1994).
    10. Not all aspects of Sellars's thought, however. Brandom sluffs off, for example,
Sellars's attempt to revive the "picturing" relation between language and world
which Wittgenstein formulated in the *Tractatus* and later repudiated, as well as his
speculations about the need for science to develop microphysical concepts adequate
to explain the phenomenology of perception. In this respect, Brandom stands to
"Empiricism and the Philosophy of Mind" as Davidson (who sluffs off what he calls
Quine's "adventitious philosophical puritanism") stands to "Two Dogmas." Both
men cultivate their respective teacher's central insight by stripping it of accidental
accretions.
    11. Brandom, *Making It Explicit*, p. xvi.

its Hegelian stage — an attempt foreshadowed in Sellars's wry description of "Empiricism and the Philosophy of Mind" as "incipient *Meditations Hegeliènnes*"[12] (sect. 20) and his reference to Hegel as "that great foe of 'immediacy'" (sect. 1).

From Hegel's point of view, taking Kant's point that intuitions without concepts are blind is the first step toward abandoning a bad philosophical habit which the British empiricists took over from Descartes — the habit of asking whether mind ever succeeds in making unmediated contact with world, and remaining skeptical about the status of knowledge-claims until such contact can be shown to exist. That habit is characteristic of philosophers who, in Brandom's terms, are "representationalist" (like Descartes and Locke) rather than "inferentialist" (like Leibniz, Kant, Frege, the later Wittgenstein, and Sellars). The former take concepts to be representations (or putative representations) of reality rather than, as Kant did, rules which specify how something is to be done. Kant's fundamental insight, Brandom says, "is that judgements and actions are to be understood to begin with in terms of the special way in which we are *responsible* for them."[13]

Following out this side of Kant's thought, rather than the side which led him to the skeptical conclusion that we could have no knowledge of things as they are in themselves, means emphasizing the passages in Kant which anticipate Hegel, Marx, Dewey, and Habermas, as opposed to those which connect Kant with his predecessors. This is the side of the *Critique of Pure Reason* which links up with Kant's "Project for

12. Sellars is alluding to Husserl's Paris lectures, published as *Meditations Cartesiennes*.
13. Brandom, *Making It Explicit*, p. 8.

a Universal History with Cosmopolitan Intent," rather than with Leibniz and Hume.

I once took the liberty of asking Sellars, "If a man chooses to bind the spirit of Hegel in the fetters of Carnap, how shall he find readers?"[14] My question was prompted by the final section of "Empiricism and the Philosophy of Mind," one of the few places where Sellars let himself go. In that section he offers a brief, but synoptic, vision of world history:

> I have used a myth [of Jones] to kill a myth—the Myth of the Given. But is my myth really a myth? Or does the reader not recognize Jones as Man himself in the middle of his journey from the grunts and groans of the cave to the subtle and polydimensional discourse of the drawing room, the laboratory, and the study, the language of Henry and William James, of Einstein and of the philosophers who, in their efforts to break out of discourse to an *arché* beyond discourse, have provided the most curious dimension of all? (sect. 63)

This question serves to link the Myth of Jones to Hegel's account, in the *Phenomenology*, of the transition from sense-perception to consciousness to self-consciousness—and, more generally, from Nature to Spirit—and also to Darwin's amendments to that account. Sellars's inclusion of Henry James as well as of Einstein reminds us of his justified suspicion of the science-worship which afflicted the early stages of analytic philosophy. The final clause serves as a rebuke to all those philosophers, from Plato to Ayer, who

14. I was attempting a pastiche of W. G. Pogson-Smith's question about Spinoza: "If a man choose to bind the spirit of Christ in the fetters of Euclid, how shall he find readers?" Sellars was not amused.

hoped to "break out of discourse,"[15] and as a reminder that the moral of the essay as a whole is that, though there is no such *arché*, we are none the worse for that.

Brandom begins, so to speak, where Sellars's essay leaves off. His book makes good on a lot of what Sellars called his "promissory notes," and it ends with a description of "the complete and explicit interpretive equilibrium exhibited by a community whose members adopt the explicit discursive stance toward each other"—an equilibrium Brandom identifies with "social self-consciousness."[16] Brandom offers a vision of all language-users forming "one great Community comprising members of all particular communities—the Community of those who say 'we' with and to someone, whether the members of those different particular communities recognize each other or not."[17]

This sort of free and easy transition between philosophy of language and mind on the one hand, and world-historical vision on the other, is reminiscent not only of Mead and Dewey but also of Gadamer and Habermas. Such transitions, as well as Sellars's and Brandom's prope-Hegelianism, suggest that the Sellars-Brandom "social practice" approach to the traditional topics of analytic philosophy might help reconnect that philosophical tradition with the so-called "Continental" tradition.

Philosophers in non-anglophone countries typically think quite hard about Hegel, whereas the rather skimpy training in the history of philosophy which most analytic philosophers

---

15. And perhaps also as a rebuke to Hegel's occasional suggestions that, at the end of inquiry and of History, we too might manage to break out of it.

16. Brandom, *Making It Explicit*, p. 643.

17. Brandom, *Making It Explicit*, p. 4.

receive often tempts them to skip straight from Kant to Frege. It is agreeable to imagine a future in which the tiresome "analytic-Continental split" is looked back upon as an unfortunate, temporary breakdown of communication—a future in which Sellars and Habermas, Davidson and Gadamer, Putnam and Derrida, Rawls and Foucault, are seen as fellow-travelers on the same journey, fellow-citizens of what Michael Oakeshott called a *civitas pelegrina*.

WILFRID SELLARS

## I. An Ambiguity in Sense-Datum Theories

I PRESUME that no philosopher who has attacked
the philosophical idea of givenness or, to use the
Hegelian term, immediacy, has intended to deny that
there is a difference between *inferring* that something
is the case and, for example, *seeing* it to be the case.
If the term "given" referred merely to what is observed as being observed, or, perhaps, to a proper
subset of the things we are said to determine by
observation, the existence of "data" would be as noncontroversial as the existence of philosophical perplexities. But, of course, this just isn't so. The phrase
"the given" as a piece of professional—epistemological—shoptalk carries a substantial theoretical commitment, and one can deny that there are "data" or that
anything is, in this sense, "given" without flying in the
face of reason.

Note: This paper was first presented as the University of London
Special Lectures on Philosophy for 1955–56, delivered on March 1, 8, and
15, 1956, under the title "The Myth of the Given: Three Lectures on
Empiricism and the Philosophy of Mind."

Many things have been said to be "given": sense contents, material objects, universals, propositions, real connections, first principles, even givenness itself. And there is, indeed, a certain way of construing the situations which philosophers analyze in these terms which can be said to be the framework of givenness. This framework has been a common feature of most of the major systems of philosophy, including, to use a Kantian turn of phrase, both "dogmatic rationalism" and "skeptical empiricism." It has, indeed, been so pervasive that few, if any, philosophers have been altogether free of it; certainly not Kant, and, I would argue, not even Hegel, that great foe of "immediacy." Often what is attacked under its name are only specific varieties of "given." Intuited first principles and synthetic necessary connections were the first to come under attack. And many who today attack "the whole idea of givenness"—and they are an increasing number—are really only attacking sense data. For they transfer to other items, say physical objects or relations of appearing, the characteristic features of the "given." If, however, I begin my argument with an attack on sense datum theories, it is only as a first step in a general critique of the entire framework of givenness.

**2.** Sense-datum theories characteristically distinguish between an *act* of awareness and, for example, the color patch which is its *object.* The act is usually called *sensing.* Classical exponents of the theory have often characterized these acts as "phenomenologically simple" and "not further analyzable." But other sense-datum theorists—some of them with an equal claim to be considered "classical exponents"—have held that sensing is analyzable. And if some philosophers seem to have thought that if sensing is analyzable, then it can't be an *act,* this has by no means been the general opinion.

There are, indeed, deeper roots for the doubt that sensing (if there is such a thing) is an act, roots which can be traced to one of two lines of thought tangled together in classical sense-datum theory. For the moment, however, I shall simply assume that however complex (or simple) the fact that x is sensed may be, it has the form, whatever exactly it may be, by virtue of which for x to be sensed is for it to be the object of an act.

Being a sense datum, or sensum, is a relational property of the item that is sensed. To refer to an item which is sensed in a way which does not entail that it *is* sensed, it is necessary to use some other locution. *Sensible* has the disadvantage that it implies that sensed items could exist without being sensed, and this is a matter of controversy among sense-datum theorists. *Sense content* is, perhaps, as neutral a term as any.

There appear to be varieties of sensing, referred to by some as *visual sensing, tactual sensing*, etc., and by others as *directly seeing, directly hearing*, etc. But it is not clear whether these are species of sensing in any full-blooded sense, or whether "x is visually sensed" amounts to no more than "x is a color patch which is sensed," "x is directly heard" than "x is a sound which is sensed" and so on. In the latter case, being a *visual sensing* or a *direct hearing* would be a relational property of an act of sensing, just as being a sense datum is a relational property of a sense content.

**3.** Now if we bear in mind that the point of the epistemological category of the given is, presumably, to explicate the idea that empirical knowledge rests on a 'foundation' of non-inferential knowledge of matter of fact, we may well experience a feeling of surprise on noting that according to sense-datum theorists, it is *particulars* that are sensed. For what is *known*, even in non-inferential knowledge, is *facts* rather than particulars, items of the form *something's being thus-and-so* or *something's standing in a certain relation to something else.* It would seem, then, that the sensing of sense contents *cannot* constitute knowledge, inferential *or* non-inferential; and if so, we may well ask, what light does the concept of a sense datum throw on the 'foundations of empirical knowledge?' The sense-datum theorist, it would seem, must choose between saying:

(a) It is *particulars* which are sensed. Sensing is not knowing. The existence of sense-data does not *logically* imply the existence of knowledge.

or

(b) Sensing *is* a form of knowing. It is *facts* rather than *particulars* which are sensed.

On alternative (a) the fact that a sense content was sensed would be a *non-epistemic* fact about the sense content. Yet it would be hasty to conclude that this alternative precludes *any* logical connection between the sensing of sense contents and the possession of non-inferential knowledge. For even if the sensing of sense contents did not logically imply the existence of non-inferential knowledge, the converse might well be true. Thus, the non-inferential knowledge of particular matter of fact might logically imply the existence of sense data (for example, *seeing that a certain physical object is red* might logically imply *sensing a red sense content*) even though the sensing of a red sense content were not itself a cognitive fact and did not imply the possession of non-inferential knowledge.

On the second alternative, (b), the sensing of sense contents would logically imply the existence of non-inferential knowledge for the simple reason that it would *be* this knowledge. But, once again, it would be facts rather than particulars which are sensed.

**4.** Now it might seem that when confronted by this choice, the sense-datum theorist seeks to have his cake and eat it. For he characteristically insists *both* that sensing is a knowing *and* that it is particulars which are sensed. Yet his position is by no means as hopeless as this formulation suggests. For the 'having' and the 'eating' *can* be combined without logical nonsense provided that he uses the word *know* and, correspondingly, the word *given* in two senses. He must say something like the following:

> The non-inferential knowing on which our world picture rests is the knowing that certain items, e.g. red sense contents, are of a certain character, e.g. red. When such a fact is non-inferentially known about a sense content, I will say that the sense content is sensed *as being,* e.g., *red.* I will then say that a sense content is *sensed* (full stop) if it is *sensed as being* of a certain character, e.g. red. Finally, I will say of a sense content that it is *known* if it is sensed (full stop), to emphasize that sensing is a *cognitive* or *epistemic* fact.

Notice that, given these stipulations, it is logically necessary that if a sense content be *sensed,* it be *sensed as being of a certain character,* and that if it be *sensed as being of a certain character,* the *fact that it is of this character* be *non-inferentially known.* Notice also that the being sensed of a sense content would be *knowledge* only in a stipulated sense of *know.* To say of a *sense content*—a color patch, for example—that it was 'known' would be to say that *some fact about it* was non-inferentially known, e.g. that it was red. This *stipulated* use of *know* would, however, receive aid and comfort from the fact that there is, in ordinary usage, a sense of *know* in which it is followed by a noun or descriptive phrase which refers to a particular, thus

Do you know John?
Do you know the President?

Because these questions are equivalent to "Are you acquainted with John?" and "Are you acquainted with the President?" the phrase "knowledge by acquaintance" recommends itself as a useful metaphor for this stipulated sense of *know* and, like other useful metaphors, has congealed into a technical term.

5. We have seen that the fact that a sense content is a *datum* (if, indeed, there are such facts) will logically imply that someone has non-inferential knowledge *only* if to say that a sense content is given is contextually defined in terms of non-inferential knowledge of a fact about this sense content. If this is not clearly realized or held in mind, sense-datum theorists may come to think of the givenness of sense contents as the *basic* or *primitive* concept of the sense-datum framework, and thus sever the logical connection between sense data and non-inferential knowledge to which the classical form of the theory is committed. This brings us face to face with the fact that in spite of the above considerations, many if not most sense-datum theorists *have* thought of the givenness of sense contents as the basic notion of the sense-datum framework. What, then, of the logical connection in the direction *sensing sense contents → having non-inferential knowledge*? Clearly it is severed by those who think of sensing as a unique and unanalyzable act. Those, on the other hand, who conceive of sensing as an *analyzable* fact, while they have prima facie severed this connection (by taking the sensing of sense contents to be the basic concept

of the sense-datum framework) will nevertheless, in a sense, have maintained it, if the result they get by analyzing *x is a red sense datum* turns out to be the same as the result they get when they analyze *x is non-inferentially known to be red*. The entailment which was thrown out the front door would have sneaked in by the back.

It is interesting to note, in this connection, that those who, in the classical period of sense-datum theories, say from Moore's "Refutation of Idealism" until about 1938, analyzed or sketched an analysis of sensing, did so in *non-epistemic* terms. Typically it was held that for a sense content to be sensed is for it to be an element in a certain kind of relational array of sense contents, where the relations which constitute the array are such relations as spatiotemporal juxtaposition (or overlapping), constant conjunction, mnemic causation—even real connection and belonging to a self. There is, however, one class of terms which is conspicuous by its absence, namely *cognitive* terms. For these, like the 'sensing' which was under analysis, were taken to belong to a higher level of complexity.

Now the idea that epistemic facts can be analyzed without remainder—even "in principle"—into non-epistemic facts, whether phenomenal or behavioral, public or private, with no matter how lavish a sprinkling of subjunctives and hypotheticals is, I believe, a radical mistake—a mistake of a piece with the so-called "naturalistic fallacy" in ethics. I shall not, however, press this point for the moment, though it will be a central theme in a later stage of my argument. What I do want to stress is that whether classical sense-datum philosophers have conceived of the givenness of sense contents as analyzable in non-epistemic terms, or as constituted by acts which are somehow both irreducible *and* knowings, they have without exception taken them to be fundamental in another sense.

**6.** For they have taken givenness to be a fact which presupposes no learning, no forming of associations, no setting up of stimulus-response connections. In short, they have tended to equate *sensing sense contents* with *being conscious*, as a person who has been hit on the head is *not* conscious whereas a new born babe, alive and kicking, *is* conscious. They would admit, of course, that the ability to know that a *person*, namely oneself, is *now*, at a certain time, feeling a pain, *is* acquired and does presuppose a (complicated) process of concept formation. But, they would insist, to suppose that the simple ability to *feel a pain* or *see a color*, in short, to sense sense contents, is *acquired* and involves a process of concept formation, would be very odd indeed.

But if a sense-datum philosopher takes the ability to sense sense contents to be unacquired, he is clearly precluded from offering an analysis of *x senses a sense content* which presupposes acquired abilities. It follows that he could analyze *x senses red sense content s* as *x non-inferentially knows that s is red* only if he is prepared to admit that the ability to have such non-inferential knowledge as that, for example, a red sense content is red, is itself unacquired. And this brings us face to face with the fact that most empirically minded philosophers are strongly inclined to think that all classificatory consciousness, all knowledge *that something is thus-and-so*, or, in logicians' jargon, all subsumption of particulars under universals, involves learning, concept formation, even the use of symbols. It is clear from the above analysis, therefore, that *classical* sense-datum theories — I emphasize the adjective, for there are other, 'heterodox,' sense-datum theories to be taken into account — are confronted by an inconsistent triad made up of the following three propositions:

A. *X senses red sense content s* entails *x non-inferentially knows that s is red.*

B. The ability to sense sense contents is unacquired.

C. The ability to know facts of the form *x is φ* is acquired.

A and B together entail not-C; B and C entail not-A; A and C entail not-B.

Once the classical sense-datum theorist faces up to the fact that A, B, and C do form an inconsistent triad, which of them will he choose to abandon?

1) He can abandon A, in which case the sensing of sense contents becomes a noncognitive fact—a non-cognitive fact, to be sure which may be a necessary condition, even a *logically* necessary condition, of non-inferential knowledge, but a fact, nevertheless, which cannot *constitute* this knowledge.

2) He can abandon B, in which case he must pay the price of cutting off the concept of a sense datum from its connection with our ordinary talk about sensations, feelings, afterimages, tickles and itches, etc., which are usually thought by sense-datum theorists to be its common sense counterparts.

3) But to abandon C is to do violence to the predominantly nominalistic proclivities of the empiricist tradition.

**7.** It certainly begins to look as though the classical concept of a sense datum were a mongrel resulting from a crossbreeding of two ideas:

(1) The idea that there are certain inner episodes—e.g. sensations of red or of C# which can occur to human beings (and brutes) without any prior process of learning or concept formation; and without which it

would *in some sense* be impossible to *see,* for example, that the facing surface of a physical object is red and triangular, or *hear* that a certain physical sound is C#.

(2) The idea that there are certain inner episodes which are the non-inferential knowings that certain items are, for example, red or C#; and that these episodes are the necessary conditions of empirical knowledge as providing the evidence for all other empirical propositions.

And I think that once we are on the lookout for them, it is quite easy to see how these two ideas came to be blended together in traditional epistemology. The *first* idea clearly arises in the attempt to explain the facts of sense perception in scientific style. How does it happen that people can have the experience which they describe by saying "It is as though I were seeing a red and triangular physical object" when either there is no physical object there at all, or, if there is, it is neither red nor triangular? The explanation, roughly, posits that in every case in which a person has an experience of this kind, whether veridical or not, he has what is called a 'sensation' or 'impression' 'of a red triangle.' The core idea is that the proximate cause of such a sensation is *only for the most part* brought about by the presence in the neighborhood of the perceiver of a red and triangular physical object; and that while a baby, say, can have the 'sensation of a red triangle' without either *seeing* or *seeming to see that the facing side of a physical object is red and triangular,* there usually *looks,* to adults, *to be* a physical object with a red and triangular facing surface, when they are caused to have a 'sensation of a red triangle'; while *without* such a sensation, no such experience can be had.

I shall have a great deal more to say about this kind of 'explanation' of perceptual situations in the course of my argument. What I want to emphasize for the moment, however, is that, as far as the above formulation goes, there is no reason to suppose that having the sensation of a red triangle is a *cognitive* or *epistemic* fact. There is, of course, a temptation to assimilate "having a sensation of a red triangle" to "thinking of a celestial city" and to attribute to the former the epistemic character, the 'intentionality' of the latter. But this temptation *could* be resisted, and it *could* be held that having a sensation of a red triangle is a fact *sui generis*, neither epistemic nor physical, having its own logical grammar. Unfortunately, the idea that there are such things as sensations of red triangles—in itself, as we shall see, quite legitimate, though not without its puzzles—seems to fit the requirements of another, and less fortunate, line of thought so well that it has almost invariably been distorted to give the latter a reinforcement without which it would long ago have collapsed. This unfortunate, but familiar, line of thought runs as follows:

> The seeing that the facing surface of a physical object is red and triangular is a *veridical* member of a class of experiences— let us call them 'ostensible seeings'—some of the members of which are non-veridical; and there is no inspectible hallmark which guarantees that *any* such experience is veridical. To suppose that the non-inferential knowledge on which our world picture rests consists of such ostensible seeings, hearings, etc., as *happen* to be veridical is to place empirical knowledge on too precarious a footing—indeed, to open the door to skepticism by making a mockery of the word *knowledge* in the phrase "empirical knowledge."

Now it is, of course, possible to delimit subclasses of ostensible seeings, hearings, etc., which are progressively less precarious, i.e. more reliable, by specifying the circumstances in which they occur, and the vigilance of the perceiver. But the possibility that any given ostensible seeing, hearing, etc., is non-veridical can never be entirely eliminated. Therefore, given that the foundation of empirical *knowledge* cannot consist of the veridical members of a class not all the members of which are veridical, and from which the non-veridical members cannot be weeded out by 'inspection,' this foundation cannot consist of such items as *seeing that the facing surface of a physical object is red and triangular.*

Thus baldly put, scarcely anyone would accept this conclusion. Rather they would take the contrapositive of the argument, and reason that *since* the foundation of empirical knowledge *is* the non-inferential knowledge of such facts, it *does* consist of members of a class which contains non-veridical members. But before it is thus baldly put, it gets tangled up with the first line of thought. The idea springs to mind that *sensations of red triangles* have exactly the virtues which *ostensible seeings of red triangular physical surfaces* lack. To begin with, the grammatical similarity of 'sensation of a red triangle' to "thought of a celestial city" is interpreted to mean, or, better, gives rise to the presupposition, that *sensations* belong in the same general pigeonhole as *thoughts*—in short, are cognitive facts. *Then*, it is noticed that sensations are *ex hypothesi* far more intimately related to mental processes than external physical objects. It would seem easier to "get at" a red triangle of which we are having a sensation, than to "get at" a red and triangular physical surface. But, above all, it is the fact that it *doesn't make sense* to speak of unveridical sensations which strikes these philosophers, though for it to strike them as it does, they must overlook the fact that if it makes sense to speak of an experience as *veridical* it must correspondingly make sense to speak of it as *unveridical.* Let me emphasize that not *all* sense-datum theorists—even of the classical type—have been guilty of *all* these confusions; nor are these *all* the confusions of which sense-datum theorists have been guilty. I shall have more to say on this topic later. But the confusions I have mentioned are central to the tradition, and will serve my present purpose. For the upshot of blending all these ingre- ⤳ dients together is the idea that a sensation of a red triangle is the very paradigm of empirical knowledge. And I think that it can readily be seen that this idea leads straight to the orthodox type of sense-datum theory and accounts for the perplexities which arise when one tries to think it through.

## II. Another Language?

**8.** I shall now examine briefly a heterodox suggestion by, for example, Ayer (1)(2) to the effect that discourse about sense data is, so to speak, another language, a language contrived by the epistemologist, for situations which the plain man describes by means of such locutions as "Now the book looks green to me" and "There seems to be a red and triangular object over there." The core of this suggestion is the idea that the vocabulary of sense data embodies no increase in the content of descriptive discourse, as over and against the plain man's language of physical objects in Space and Time, and the properties they have and appear to have. For it holds that sentences of the form

$$X \text{ presents } S \text{ with a } \phi \text{ sense datum}$$

are simply *stipulated* to have the same force as sentences of the form

X looks φ to S.

Thus "The tomato presents S with a bulgy red sense-datum" would be the contrived counterpart of "The tomato looks red and bulgy to S" and would mean exactly what the latter means for the simple reason that it was stipulated to do so.

As an aid to explicating this suggestion, I am going to make use of a certain picture. I am going to start with the idea of a *code*, and I am going to enrich this notion until the codes I am talking about are no longer *mere* codes. Whether one wants to call these "enriched codes" codes at all is a matter which I shall not attempt to decide.

Now a code, in the sense in which I shall use the term, is a system of symbols each of which represents a complete sentence. Thus, as we initially view the situation, there are two characteristic features of a code: (1) Each code symbol is a unit; the parts of a code symbol are not themselves code symbols. (2) Such logical relations as obtain among code symbols are completely parasitical; they derive entirely from logical relations among the sentences they represent. Indeed, to speak about logical relations among code symbols is a way of talking which is introduced in terms of the logical relations among the sentences they represent. Thus, if "○" stands for "Everybody on board is sick" and "△" for "Somebody on board is sick," then "△" would follow from "○" in the sense that the sentence represented by "△" follows from the sentence represented by "○."

Let me begin to modify this austere conception of a code. There is no reason why a code symbol might not have parts which, without becoming full-fledged symbols on their own, do play a role in the system. Thus they might play the role of *mnemonic devices* serving to put us in mind of features of the sentences represented by the symbols of which they are parts. For example, the code symbol for "Someone on board is sick" might contain the letter S to remind us of the word "sick," and, perhaps, the reversed letter E to remind those of us who have a background in logic of the word "someone." Thus, the flag for "Someone on board is sick" might be '∃S.' Now the suggestion at which I am obviously driving is that someone might introduce so-called sense-datum sentences as code symbols or "flags," and introduce the vocables and printables they contain to serve the role of reminding us of certain features of the sentences in ordinary perceptual discourse which the flags as wholes represent. In particular, the role of the vocable or printable "sense datum" would be that of indicating that the symbolized sentence contains the context ". . . looks . . . ," the vocable or printable "red" that the correlated sentence contains the context ". . . looks red . . ." and so on.

**9.** Now to take this conception of sense datum 'sentences' seriously is, of course, to take seriously the idea that there are no independent logical relations between sense-datum 'sentences.' It *looks* as though there were such independent logical relations, for these 'sentences' look like *sentences*, and they have as proper parts vocables or printables which function *in ordinary usage* as *logical words*. Certainly if sense-datum talk is a code, it is a code which is easily mistaken for a language proper. Let me illustrate. At first sight it certainly seems that

A. The tomato presents S with a red sense datum

entails both

B. There are red sense data

and

C. The tomato presents S with a sense datum which has some specific shade of red.

This, however, on the kind of view I am considering, would be a mistake. (B) would follow—even in the inverted commas sense of 'follows' appropriate to code symbols—from (A) only because (B) is the flag for (β), "Something looks red to somebody," which *does* follow from (α), "The tomato looks red to Jones" which is represented in the code by (A). And (C) would 'follow' from (A), in spite of appearances, only if (C) were the flag for a *sentence* which *follows* from (α).

I shall have more to say about this example in a moment. The point to be stressed now is that to carry out this view consistently one must deny to such vocables and printables as "quality," "is," "red," "color," "crimson," "determinable," "determinate," "all," "some," "exists," etc., etc., *as they occur in sense-datum talk,* the full-blooded status of their counterparts in ordinary usage. They are rather *clues* which serve to remind us which sense-datum 'flag' it would be proper to fly along with which other sense-datum 'flags.' Thus, the vocables which make up the two 'flags'

(D) All sense-data are red

and

(E) Some sense data are not red

remind us of the genuine logical incompatibility between, for example,

(F) All elephants are grey

and

(G) Some elephants are not grey,

and serve, therefore, as a clue to the impropriety of flying these two 'flags' together. For the sentences they symbolize are, presumably,

(δ) Everything looks red to everybody

and

(ε) There is a color other than red which something looks to somebody to have,

and these *are* incompatible.

But one would have to be cautious in using these clues. Thus, from the fact that it is proper to infer

(H) Some elephants have a determinate shade of pink

from

(I) Some elephants are pink

it would clearly be a mistake to infer that the right to fly

(K) Some sense data are pink

carries with it the right to fly

(L) Some sense data have a determinate shade of pink.

9. But if sense-datum sentences are really sense-datum 'sentences'—i.e. code flags—it follows, of course, that sense-datum talk neither *clarifies* nor *explains* facts of the form *x looks φ to S* or *x is φ*. That it would appear to do so would be because it would take an almost superhuman effort to keep from taking the vocables and printables which occur in the code (and let me now add to our earlier list the vocable "directly known") to be *words* which, if homonyms of words in ordinary usage, have their ordinary sense, and which, if invented, have a meaning specified by their relation to the others. One would be constantly tempted, that is, to treat sense-datum flags as though they were sentences in a *theory*, and sense-datum talk as a *language* which gets its use by coordinating sense-datum sentences with sentences in ordinary perception talk, *as molecule talk gets its use by coordinating*

*sentences about populations of molecules with talk about the pressure
of gases on the walls of their containers.* After all,

   x looks red to S $\cdot \equiv \cdot$ there is a class of red sense data
         which belong to x, and are sensed by S

has at least a superficial resemblance to

   g exerts pressure on w $\cdot \equiv \cdot$ there is a class of molecules
         which make up g, and which are bouncing off w,

a resemblance which becomes even more striking once it is
granted that the former is not an *analysis* of *x looks red to S*
in terms of sense data.

   There is, therefore, reason to believe that it is the fact that
both codes and theories are contrived systems which are
under the control of the language with which they are coordinated, which has given aid and comfort to the idea that
sense-datum talk is "another language" for ordinary discourse about perception. Yet although the logical relations
between sentences in a theoretical language are, in an important sense, under the control of logical relations between
sentences in the observation language, nevertheless, within
the framework of this control, the theoretical language has
an *autonomy* which contradicts the very idea of a code. If
this essential difference between theories and codes is over-
looked, one may be tempted to try to eat his cake and have
it. By thinking of sense-datum talk as *merely another language,*
one draws on the fact that codes have no surplus value.
By thinking of sense-datum talk as *illuminating* the "language
of appearing," one draws on the fact that theoretical lan-
guages, though *contrived*, and depending for their meaningfulness on a coordination with the language of observation, have
an explanatory function. Unfortunately, these two charac-

teristics are incompatible; for it is just because theories have "surplus value" that they can provide explanations.

No one, of course, who thinks—as, for example, does Ayer—of the existence of sense data as entailing the existence of "direct knowledge," would wish to say that sense *data* are theoretical entities. It could scarcely be a theoretical fact that I am directly knowing that a certain sense content is red. On the other hand, the idea that sense *contents* are theoretical entities is not *obviously* absurd—so absurd as to preclude the above interpretation of the plausibility of the "another-language" approach. For even those who introduce the expression "sense content" by means of the context ". . . is directly known to be . . ." may fail to keep this fact in mind when putting this expression to use—for example, by developing the idea that physical objects and persons alike are patterns of sense contents. In such a specific context, it is possible to forget that sense *contents*, thus introduced, are essentially sense *data* and not merely items which exemplify sense qualities. Indeed, one may even lapse into thinking of the *sensing* of sense contents, the givenness of sense *data*, as *non-epistemic* facts.

I think it fair to say that those who offer the "another-language" interpretation of sense data find the illumination it provides to consist primarily in the fact that in the language of sense data, physical objects are patterns of sense contents, so that, viewed in this framework, there is no "iron curtain" between the knowing mind and the physical world. It is to elaborating plausible (if schematic) translations of physical-object statements into statements about sense contents, rather than to spelling out the force of such sentences as "Sense content *s* is directly known to be red," that the greater part of their philosophical ingenuity has been directed.

However this may be, one thing can be said with confidence. If the language of sense data *were* merely a code, a notational device, then the cash value of any philosophical clarification it might provide must lie in its ability to illuminate logical relations *within* ordinary discourse about physical objects and our perception of them. Thus, the fact (if it were a fact) that a code can be constructed for ordinary perception talk which 'speaks' of a "relation of identity" between the components ("sense data") of "minds" and of "things," would presumably have as its cash value the insight that ordinary discourse about physical objects and perceivers could (in principle) be constructed from sentences of the form "There looks to be a physical object with a red and triangular facing surface over there" (the counterpart in ordinary language of the basic expressions of the code). In more traditional terms, the clarification would consist in making manifest the fact that persons and things are alike logical constructions out of *lookings* or *appearings* (*not* appearances!). But any claim to this effect soon runs into insuperable difficulties which become apparent once the role of "looks" or "appears" is understood. And it is to an examination of this role that I now turn.

## III. The Logic of 'Looks'

**10.** Before turning aside to examine the suggestion that the language of sense data is "another language" for the situations described by the so-called "language of appearing," I had concluded that classical sense-datum theories, when pressed, reveal themselves to be the result of a mismating of two ideas: (1) The idea that there are certain "inner episodes," e.g. the sensation of a red triangle or of a C# sound, which occur to human beings and brutes without any prior process of learning or concept formation, and without which it would—in *some* sense—be impossible to *see*, for example, that the facing surface of a physical object is red and triangular, or *hear* that a certain physical sound is C#; (2) The idea that there are certain "inner episodes" which are the noninferential knowings that, for example, a certain item is red and triangular, or, in the case of sounds, C#, which inner episodes are the necessary conditions of empirical knowledge as providing the evidence for all other empirical propositions. If this diagnosis is correct, a reasonable next step would be to examine these two ideas and determine how that which survives criticism in each is properly to be combined with the other. Clearly we would have to come to grips with the idea of *inner episodes*, for this is common to both.

Many who attack the idea of the given seem to have thought that the central mistake embedded in this idea is exactly the idea that there are inner episodes, whether thoughts or so-called "immediate experiences," to which each of us has privileged access. I shall argue that this is just not so, and that the Myth of the Given can be dispelled without resorting to the crude verificationisms or operationalisms characteristic of the more dogmatic forms of recent empiricism. Then there are those who, while they do not reject the idea of inner episodes, find the Myth of the Given to consist in the idea that knowledge of these episodes furnishes *premises* on which empirical knowledge rests as on a foundation. But while this idea has, indeed, been the most widespread form of the Myth, it is far from constituting its essence. Everything hinges on *why* these philosophers reject it. If, for example, it is on the ground that the learning of a language is a *public* process which proceeds in a domain of *public* objects and is governed by *public* sanctions, so that *private* episodes—with the exception of a mysterious nod in their direction—must needs escape the net of rational discourse, then, while these philosophers are immune to the form of the myth which has flowered in sense-datum theories, they have no defense against the myth in the form of the givenness of such facts as that *physical object x looks red to person S at time t,* or that *there looks to person S at time t to be a red physical object over there.* It will be useful to pursue the Myth in this direction for a while before more general issues are raised.

**11.** Philosophers have found it easy to suppose that such a sentence as "The tomato looks red to Jones" says that a certain triadic relation, *looking* or *appearing,* obtains among a physical object, a person, and a quality.* "A looks $\phi$ to S" is assimilated to "x gives y to z"—or, better, since giving is, strictly speaking, an action rather than a relation—to "x is between y and z," and taken to be a case of the general form "R(x,y,z)." Having supposed this, they turn without further ado to the question, "Is this relation analyzable?" Sense-datum theorists have, on the whole, answered "Yes," and claimed that facts of the form *x looks red to X* are to be analyzed in terms of sense data. Some of them, without necessarily rejecting this claim, have argued that facts of this kind are, at the very least, to be *explained* in terms of sense data. Thus, when Broad (4) writes "If, in fact, nothing elliptical is before my mind, it is very hard to understand why the penny should seem *elliptical* rather than of any other shape (p. 240)," he is appealing to sense-data as a means of *explaining* facts of this form. The difference, of course, is that

---

* A useful discussion of views of this type is to be found in (9) and (13).

whereas if *x looks* φ *to S* is correctly *analyzed* in terms of sense data, then no one could believe that x looks φ to S without believing that S has sense data, the same need not be true if *x looks* φ *to S* is explained in terms of sense data, for, in the case of some types of explanation, at least, one can believe a fact without believing its explanation.

On the other hand, those philosophers who reject sense-datum theories in favor of so-called theories of appearing have characteristically held that facts of the form *x looks* φ *to S* are ultimate and irreducible, and that sense data are needed neither for their analysis nor for their explanation. If asked, "Doesn't the statement 'x looks red to S' have as part of its meaning the idea that s stands in some relation to something that *is* red?" their answer is in the negative, and, I believe, rightly so.

**12.** I shall begin my examination of "X looks red to S at t" with the simple but fundamental point that the sense of "red" in which things *look* red is, on the face of it, the same as that in which things *are* red. When one glimpses an object and decides that it looks red (to *me*, *now*, from here) and wonders whether it really *is* red, one is surely wondering whether the color—red—which it looks to have is the one it really does have. This point can be obscured by such verbal manipulations as hyphenating the words "looks" and "red" and claiming that it is the insoluble unity "looks-red" and not just "looks" which is the relation. Insofar as this dodge is based on insight, it is insight into the fact that *looks* is not a relation between a person, a thing, and a quality. Unfortunately, as we shall see, the reason for this fact is one which gives no comfort at all to the idea that it is *looks-red* rather than *looks* which is the relation.

I have, in effect, been claiming that *being red* is logically prior, is a logically simpler notion, than *looking red;* the function "x is red" to "x looks red to y." In short, that it just won't do to say that *x is red* is analyzable in terms of *x looks red to y.* But what, then, are we to make of the necessary truth — and it is, of course, a necessary truth — that

x *is* red ·≡· x would *look* red to standard observers
in standard conditions?

There is certainly some sense to the idea that this is at least the schema for a definition of *physical redness* in terms of *looking red.* One begins to see the plausibility of the gambit that *looking-red* is an insoluble unity, for the minute one gives "red" (on the right-hand side) an independent status, it becomes what it obviously is, namely "red" as a predicate of physical objects, and the supposed definition becomes an obvious circle.

**13.** The way out of this troubling situation has two parts. The *second* is to show how "x *is* red" can be necessarily equivalent to "x would *look* red to standard observers in standard situations" without this being a definition of "x is red" in terms of "x looks red." But the *first,* and logically prior, step is to show that "x looks red to S" does not assert either an unanalyzable triadic relation to obtain between x, red, and S, or an unanalyzable dyadic relation to obtain between x and S. Not, however, because it asserts an *analyzable* relation to obtain, but because *looks* is not a relation at all. Or, to put the matter in a familiar way, one can say that *looks* is a relation if he likes, for the sentences in which this word appears show some grammatical analogies to sentences built around words which we should not hesitate to classify as relation words; but once one has become aware of certain

other features which make them very unlike ordinary relation sentences, he will be less inclined to view his task as that
of *finding the answer* to the question "Is looks a relation?"

**14.** To bring out the essential features of the use of "looks,"
I shall engage in a little historical fiction. A young man,
whom I shall call John, works in a necktie shop. He has
learned the use of color words in the usual way, with this
exception. I shall suppose that he has never looked at an
object in other than standard conditions. As he examines his
stock every evening before closing up shop, he says, "This is
red," "That is green," "This is purple," etc., and such of his
linguistic peers as happen to be present nod their heads
approvingly.

Let us suppose, now, that at this point in the story, electric
lighting is invented. His friends and neighbors rapidly adopt
this new means of illumination, and wrestle with the problems it presents. John, however, is the last to succumb. Just
after it has been installed in his shop, one of his neighbors,
Jim, comes in to buy a necktie.

"Here is a handsome green one," says John.

"But it *isn't* green," says Jim, and takes John outside.

"Well," says John, "it was green in there, but now it is
blue."

"No," says Jim, "you know that neckties don't change
their color merely as a result of being taken from place to
place."

"But perhaps electricity changes their color and they
change back again in daylight?"

"That would be a queer kind of change, wouldn't it?" says
Jim.

"I suppose so," says bewildered John. "But we *saw* that it
was green *in there*."

"No, we didn't see that it was green in there, because it wasn't green, and you can't see what isn't so!"

"Well, this is a pretty pickle," says John. *"I just don't know what to say."*

The next time John picks up this tie in his shop and someone asks what color it is, his first impulse is to say "It is green." He suppresses this impulse, and, remembering what happened before, comes out with "It is blue." He doesn't *see* that it is blue, nor would he say that he sees it to be blue. What does he see? Let us ask him.

"I don't know *what* to say. If I didn't know that the tie is blue — and the alternative to granting this is odd indeed — I would swear that I was seeing a green tie and seeing that it is green. It is *as though* I were seeing the necktie to be green."

If we bear in mind that such sentences as "This is green" have both a *fact-stating* and a *reporting* use, we can put the point I have just been making by saying that once John learns to stifle the *report* "This necktie is green" when looking at it in the shop, there is no other *report* about color and the necktie which he knows how to make. To be sure, he now says, "This necktie is blue." But he is not making a *reporting* use of this sentence. He uses it as the conclusion of an inference.

**15.** We return to the shop after an interval, and we find that when John is asked "What is the color of this necktie?" he makes such statements as "It looks green, but take it outside and see." It occurs to us that perhaps in learning to say "This tie *looks* green" when in the shop, he has learned to make a new kind of report. Thus, it might seem as though his linguistic peers have helped him to notice a new kind of *objective* fact, one which, though a relational fact involving a perceiver, is as logically independent of the beliefs, the conceptual framework of the perceiver, as the fact that the necktie is blue; but a *minimal* fact, one which it is safer to report because one is less likely to be mistaken. Such a minimal fact would be the fact that the necktie looks green to John on a certain occasion, and it would be properly reported by using the sentence "This necktie *looks* green." It is this type of account, of course, which I have already rejected.

But what is the alternative? If, that is, we are not going to adopt the sense-datum analysis. Let me begin by noting that there certainly seems to be something to the idea that the sentence "This looks green to me now" has a reporting role. Indeed, it would seem to be essentially a report. But if so, *what* does it report, if not a minimal objective fact, and if what it reports is not to be analyzed in terms of sense data?

**16.** Let me next call attention to the fact that the experience of having something look green to one at a certain time is, insofar as it is an experience, obviously very much like that of seeing something to be green, insofar as the latter is an experience. But the latter, of course, is not *just* an experience. And this is the heart of the matter. For to say that a certain experience is a *seeing that* something is the case, is to do more than describe the experience. It is to characterize it as, so to speak, making an assertion or claim, and—which is the point I wish to stress—to *endorse* that claim. As a matter of fact, as we shall see, it is much more easy to see that the statement "Jones sees that the tree is green" ascribes a propositional claim to Jones' experience and endorses it, than to specify how the statement *describes* Jones' experience.

I realize that by speaking of experiences as containing propositional claims, I may seem to be knocking at closed doors. I ask the reader to bear with me, however, as the

justification of this way of talking is one of my major aims.
If I am permitted to issue this verbal currency now, I hope
to put it on the gold standard before concluding the argument.

**16.** It is clear that the experience of seeing that something
is green is not *merely* the occurrence of the propositional
claim 'this is green'—not even if we add, as we must, that
this claim is, so to speak, evoked or wrung from the perceiver
by the object perceived. Here Nature—to turn Kant's simile
(which he uses in another context) on its head—puts us to
the question. The something more is clearly what philosophers have in mind when they speak of "visual impressions"
or "immediate visual experiences." What exactly is the logical
status of these "impressions" or "immediate experiences" is a
problem which will be with us for the remainder of this
argument. For the moment it is the propositional claim which
concerns us.

I pointed out above that when we use the word "see" as
in "S sees that the tree is green" we are not only ascribing a
claim to the experience, but endorsing it. It is this endorsement which Ryle has in mind when he refers to *seeing that
something is thus and so* as an *achievement,* and to "sees" as an
*achievement word.* I prefer to call it a "so it is" or "just so" word,
for the root idea is that of *truth.* To characterize S's experience as a *seeing* is, in a suitably broad sense—which I shall
be concerned to explicate—to apply the semantical concept
of truth to that experience.

Now the suggestion I wish to make is, in its simplest terms,
that the statement "X looks green to Jones" differs from
"Jones sees that x is green" in that whereas the latter both
ascribes a propositional claim to Jones' experience *and endorses it,* the former ascribes the claim but does not endorse

it. This is the essential difference between the two, for it is clear that two experiences may be identical *as experiences*, and yet one be properly referred to as a *seeing that* something is green, and the other *merely* as a case of something's *looking* green. Of course, if I say "X *merely looks* green to S" I am not only failing to endorse the claim, I am rejecting it.

Thus, when I say "X looks green to me now" I am *reporting* the fact that my experience is, so to speak, intrinsically, *as an experience*, indistinguishable from a veridical one of seeing that x is green. Involved in the report is the ascription to my experience of the claim 'x is green'; and the fact that I make this report rather than the simple report "X is green" indicates that certain considerations have operated to raise, so to speak in a higher court, the question 'to endorse or not to endorse.' I may have reason to think that x may not after all be green.

If I make at one time the report "X looks to be green"—which is not only a report, but the withholding of an endorsement—I may later, when the original reasons for withholding endorsement have been rebutted, endorse the original claim by saying "I saw that it was green, though at the time I was only sure that it looked green." Notice that I will only say "I see that x is green" (as opposed to "X is green") when the question "to endorse or not to endorse" has come up. "I see that x is green" belongs, so to speak, on the same level as "X looks green" and "X merely *looks* green."

**17.** There are many interesting and subtle questions about the dialectics of "looks talk," into which I do not have the space to enter. Fortunately, the above distinctions suffice for our present purposes. Let us suppose, then, that to say that "X looks green to S at t" is, in effect, to say that S has that kind of experience which, if one were prepared to endorse the propositional claim it involves, one would characterize as *seeing x to be green at t.* Thus, when our friend John learns to use the sentence "This necktie looks green to me" he learns a way of reporting an experience of the kind which, as far as any categories I have yet permitted him to have are concerned, he can only characterize by saying that as an experience it does not differ from seeing something to be green, and that evidence for the proposition 'This necktie is green' is *ipso facto* evidence for the proposition that the experience in question is *seeing that the necktie is green.*

Now one of the chief merits of this account is that it permits a parallel treatment of 'qualitative' and 'existential' seeming or looking. Thus, when I say "The tree looks bent" I am endorsing that part of the claim involved in my experience which concerns the existence of the tree, but withholding endorsement from the rest. On the other hand, when I say "There looks to be a bent tree over there" I am refusing to endorse any but the most general aspect of the claim, namely, that there is an 'over there' as opposed to a 'here.' Another merit of the account is that it explains how a necktie, for example, can look red to S at t, without looking scarlet or crimson or any other determinate shade of red. In short it explains how things can have a *merely generic* look, a fact which would be puzzling indeed if looking red were a *natural* as opposed to *epistemic* fact about objects. The core of the explanation, of course, is that the propositional claim involved in such an experience may be, for example, either the more determinable claim 'This is red' or the more determinate claim 'This is crimson.' The complete story is more complicated, and requires some account of the role in these experiences of the 'impressions' or 'immediate experiences' the logical status of which remains to be determined. But even in the absence of these additional details, we can note the resemblance between the fact that x can look red to S, without it being true of some specific shade of red that x looks to S to be of that shade, and the fact that S can believe that Cleopatra's Needle is tall, without its being true of some determinate number of feet that S believes it to be that number of feet tall.

**18.** The point I wish to stress at this time, however, is that the concept of *looking green,* the ability to recognize that something *looks green,* presupposes the concept of *being green,* and that the latter concept involves the ability to tell what colors objects have by looking at them—which, in turn, involves knowing in what circumstances to place an object if one wishes to ascertain its color by looking at it. Let me develop this latter point. As our friend John becomes more and more sophisticated about his own and other people's visual experiences, he learns under what conditions it is as though one were seeing a necktie to be of one color when in fact it is of another. Suppose someone asks him "Why does this tie look green to me?" John may very well reply "Because it is blue, and blue objects look green in this kind of light." And if someone asks this question when looking at the necktie in plain daylight, John may very well reply "Because the tie *is* green"—to which he may add "We are in plain daylight, *and in daylight things look what they are.*" We thus see that

$$x \text{ is red } \cdot \equiv \cdot \ x \text{ looks red to standard observers in}$$
$$\text{standard conditions}$$

is a necessary truth *not* because the right-hand side is the definition of "x is red," but because "standard conditions" means conditions in which things look what they are. And, of course, *which* conditions are standard for a given mode of perception is, at the common-sense level, specified by a list of conditions which exhibit the vagueness and open texture characteristic of ordinary discourse.

**19.** I have arrived at a stage in my argument which is, at least prima facie, out of step with the basic presuppositions of logical atomism. Thus, as long as *looking green* is taken to be the notion to which *being green* is reducible, it could be claimed with considerable plausibility that fundamental concepts pertaining to observable fact have that logical independence of one another which is characteristic of the empiricist tradition. Indeed, at first sight the situation is *quite* disquieting, for if the ability to recognize that x looks green presupposes the concept of *being green,* and if this in turn involves knowing in what circumstances to view an object to ascertain its color, then, since one can scarcely determine what the circumstances are without noticing that certain objects have certain perceptible characteristics—including colors—it would seem that one couldn't form the concept of *being green,* and, by parity of reasoning, of the other colors, unless he already had them.

Now, it just won't do to reply that to have the concept of green, to know what it is for something to be green, it is sufficient to respond, when one is *in point of fact* in standard conditions, to green objects with the vocable "This is green." Not only must the conditions be of a sort that is appropriate for determining the color of an object by looking, the subject must *know* that conditions of this sort *are* appropriate. And while this does not imply that one must have concepts before one has them, it does imply that one can have the concept of green only by having a whole battery of concepts of which it is one element. It implies that while the process of acquiring the concept green may—indeed does—involve a long history of acquiring *piecemeal* habits of response to various objects in various circumstances, there is an important sense in which one has *no* concept pertaining to the observable properties of physical objects in Space and Time unless one has them all—and, indeed, as we shall see, a great deal more besides.

**20.** Now, I think it is clear what a logical atomist, supposing that he found any merit at all in the above argument, would say. He would say that I am overlooking the fact that the logical space of physical objects in Space and Time rests on the logical space of sense contents, and he would argue that it is concepts pertaining to sense contents which have the logical independence of one another which is characteristic of traditional empiricism. "After all," he would point out, "concepts pertaining to theoretical entities—molecules, for example—have the mutual dependence you have, perhaps rightly, ascribed to concepts pertaining to *physical* fact. But," he would continue, "theoretical concepts have empirical content because they rest on—are coordinated with—a more fundamental logical space. Until you have disposed, therefore, of the idea that there is a more fundamental logical space than that of physical objects in Space and Time, or shown that it too is fraught with coherence, your incipient *Meditations Hegeliènnes* are premature."

And we can imagine a sense-datum theorist to interject the following complaint: "You have begun to write as though you had shown not only that *physical redness* is not to be analyzed in terms of *looking red*—which I will grant—but also that physical redness is not to be analyzed at all, and, in particular, not to be analyzed in terms of the redness of red sense contents. Again, you have begun to write as though you had shown not only that observing that x *looks* red is not more basic than observing that x *is* red, but also that there is *no* form of visual noticing more basic than seeing that x is red, such as the sensing of a red sense content. I grant," he continues, "that the tendency of sense-datum theorists has been to claim that the *redness* of physical objects is to be analyzed in terms of *looking red*, and *then* to claim that *looking red* is itself to be analyzed in terms of *red sense contents*, and that you may have undercut this line of analysis. But what is to prevent the sense-datum theorist from taking the line that the properties of physical objects are *directly* analyzable into the qualities and phenomenal relations of sense contents?"

Very well. But once again we must ask, How does the sense-datum theorist come by the framework of sense contents? and How is he going to convince us that there are such things? For even if *looking red* doesn't enter into the analysis of physical redness, it is by asking us to reflect on the experience of having something look red to us that he hopes to make this framework convincing. And it therefore becomes relevant to note that my analysis of *x looks red to S at t* has not, at least as far as I have pushed it to date, revealed any such items as sense-contents. And it may be relevant to suggest that once we see clearly that physical redness is not to be given a dispositional analysis in terms of *looking red*, the idea that it is to be given *any* kind of dispositional analysis loses a large measure of its plausibility. In any event, the next move must be to press further the above account of qualitative and existential looking.

## IV. Explaining Looks

**21.** I have already noted that sense-datum theorists are impressed by the question "How can a physical object look red to S, unless something in that situation *is* red and S is taking account of it? If S isn't experiencing something red, how does it happen that the physical object looks *red*, rather than green or streaky?" There is, I propose to show, *something* to this line of thought, though the story turns out to be a complicated one. And if, in the course of telling the story, I shall be led to make statements which resemble *some* of the things sense-datum theorists have said, this story will amount to a sense-datum theory only in a sense which robs this phrase of an entire dimension of its traditional epistemological force, a dimension which is characteristic of even such heterodox forms of sense-datum theory as the "another language" approach.

Let me begin by formulating the question: "Is the fact that an object looks to S to be red and triangular, or that there looks to S to be a red and triangular object over there, to be explained in terms of the idea that Jones has a sensation — or impression, or immediate experience — of a red triangle? One point can be made right away, namely that if these expressions are so understood that, say, the immediate experience of a red triangle implies the existence of something — not a physical object — which *is* red and triangular, and if the redness which this item has is the same as the redness which the physical object *looks* to have, then the suggestion runs up against the objection that the redness physical objects *look* to have is the same as the redness physical objects actually *do* have, so that items which *ex hypothesi* are not physical objects, and which radically, even categorically, differ from physical objects, would have the same redness as physical objects. And while this is, perhaps, not entirely out of the question, it certainly provides food for thought. Yet when it is claimed that "obviously" physical objects can't *look* red to one unless one is experiencing something that *is* red, is it not presumed that the redness which the *something* has is the redness which the physical object *looks to have*?

Now there are those who would say that the question "Is the fact that an object looks red and triangular to S to be explained—as opposed to notationally reformulated—in terms of the idea that S has an impression of a red triangle?" simply doesn't arise, on the ground that there are perfectly sound explanations of qualitative and existential lookings which make no reference to 'immediate experiences' or other dubious entities. Thus, it is pointed out, it is perfectly proper to answer the question "Why does this object look red?" by saying "Because it is an orange object looked at in such and such circumstances." The explanation is, in principle, a good one, and is typical of the answers we make to such questions in everyday life. But because these explanations are good, it by no means follows that explanations of other kinds might not be equally good, and, perhaps, more searching.

**22.** On the face of it there are at least two ways in which additional, but equally legitimate explanations *might* be forthcoming for such a fact as that *x looks red*. The first of these is suggested by a simple analogy. Might it not be the case that just as there are two kinds of good explanation of the fact that this balloon has expanded, (a) in terms of the Boyle-Charles laws which relate the empirical concepts of volume, pressure, and temperature pertaining to gases, and (b) in terms of the kinetic theory of gases; so there are two ways of explaining the fact that this object looks red to S: (a) in terms of empirical generalizations relating the colors of objects, the circumstances in which they are seen, and the colors they look to have, and (b) in terms of a theory of perception in which 'immediate experiences' play a role analogous to that of the molecules of the kinetic theory.

Now there is such an air of paradox to the idea that 'immediate experiences' are *mere* theoretical entities—entities, that is, which are postulated, along with certain fundamental principles concerning them, to explain uniformities pertaining to sense perception, as molecules, along with the principles of molecular motion, are postulated to explain the experimentally determined regularities pertaining to gases— that I am going to lay it aside until a more propitious context of thought may make it seem relevant. Certainly, those who have thought that qualitative and existential lookings are to be explained in terms of 'immediate experiences' thought of the latter as the most untheoretical of entities, indeed, as *the* observables *par excellence.*

Let us therefore turn to a second way in which, at least prima facie, there might be an additional, but equally legitimate explanation of existential and qualitative lookings. According to this second account, when we consider items of this kind, we *find* that they contain as components items which are properly referred to as, for example, 'the immediate experience of a red triangle.' Let us begin our exploration of this suggestion by taking another look at our account of existential and qualitative lookings. It will be remembered that our account of qualitative looking ran, in rough and ready terms, as follows:

> 'x looks red to S' has the sense of 'S has an experience which involves in a unique way the idea *that x is red* and involves it in such a way that if this idea were true, the experience would correctly be characterized as a seeing that x is red.'

Thus, our account implies that the three situations

(a) Seeing that x, over there, is red
(b) Its looking to one that x, over there, is red

(c) Its looking to one as though there were a red object
over there

differ primarily in that (a) is so formulated as to involve an
endorsement of the idea that x, over there, is red, whereas
in (b) this idea is only partially endorsed, and in (c) not at
all. Let us refer to the idea *that x, over there, is red* as the
*common propositional content* of these three situations. (This is,
of course, not strictly correct, since the propositional content
of (c) is *existential*, rather than about a presupposedly desig-
nated object x, but it will serve my purpose. Furthermore,
the common propositional content of these three experiences
is much more complex and determinate than is indicated by
the sentence we use to describe our experience to others, and
which I am using to represent it. Nevertheless it is clear that,
subject to the first of these qualifications, the propositional
content of these three experiences *could* be identical.)

The propositional content of these three experiences is, of
course, but a part of that to which we are logically committed
by characterizing them as situations of these three kinds. Of
the remainder, as we have seen, part is a matter of the extent
to which this propositional content is endorsed. It is the
residue with which we are now concerned. Let us call this
residue the *descriptive content*. I can then point out that it is
implied by my account that not only the *propositional content*,
but also the *descriptive content* of these three experiences may
be identical. I shall suppose this to be the case, though that
there must be some factual difference in the *total* situations
is obvious.

Now, and this is the decisive point, in characterizing these
three experiences as, respectively, a *seeing that x, over there, is
red, its looking to one as though x, over there, were red*, and *its looking*

*to one as though there were a red object over there*, we do not specify this common *descriptive* content save *indirectly*, by implying that *if the common propositional content were true*, then all these three situations would be cases of *seeing* that x, over there, is red. Both existential and qualitative lookings are experiences that would be *seeings* if their propositional contents were true.

Thus, the very nature of "looks talk" is such as to raise questions to which it gives no answer: What is the *intrinsic* character of the common descriptive content of these three experiences? and How are they able to have it in spite of the fact that whereas in the case of (a) the perceiver must be in the presence of a red object over there, in (b) the object over there need not be red, while in (c) there need be no object over there at all?

**23.** Now it is clear that if we were required to give a more direct characterization of the common descriptive content of these experiences, we would begin by trying to do so in terms of the quality *red*. Yet, as I have already pointed out, we can scarcely say that this descriptive content is itself something red unless we can pry the term "red" loose from its prima-facie tie with the category of physical objects. And there is a line of thought which has been one of the standard gambits of perceptual epistemology and which seems to promise exactly this. If successful, it would convince us that *redness* — in the most basic sense of this term — is a characteristic of items of the sort we have been calling sense contents. It runs as follows:

> While it would, indeed, be a howler to say that we don't see chairs, tables, etc., but only their facing surfaces, nevertheless, although we see a table, say, and although the table has a back as well as a front, we do not see the back of the table

as we see its front. Again, although we see the table, and although the table has an 'inside,' we do not see the inside of the table as we see its facing outside. Seeing an object entails seeing its facing surface. If we are seeing that an object is red, this entails seeing that its facing surface is red. A red surface is a two-dimensional red expanse—two-dimensional in that though it may be *bulgy,* and in *this* sense three-dimensional, it has no *thickness.* As far as the analysis of perceptual consciousness is concerned, a red physical object is one that has a red expanse as its surface.

Now a red expanse is not a physical object, nor does the existence of a red expanse entail the existence of a physical object to which it belongs. (Indeed, there are "wild" expanses which do not belong to any physical object.) The "descriptive content"—as you put it—which is common to the three experiences (a), (b) and (c) above, is exactly this sort of thing, a bulgy red expanse.

Spelled out thus baldly, the fallacy is, or should be, obvious; it is a simple equivocation on the phrase "having a red surface." We start out by thinking of the familiar fact that a physical object may be of one color "on the surface" and of another color "inside." We may express this by saying that, for example, the 'surface' of the object is red, but its 'inside' green. But in saying this we are *not* saying that there is a 'surface' in the sense of a bulgy two-dimensional particular, a red 'expanse' which is a component particular in a complex particular which also includes green particulars. The notion of two-dimensional bulgy (or flat) particulars is a product of philosophical (and mathematical) sophistication which can be *related to* our ordinary conceptual framework, but does not belong in an *analysis* of it. I think that in its place it has an important contribution to make. (See below, Section 61, (5), pp. 113–115.) But this place is in the logical space of an ideal *scientific* picture of the world and not in the logical space of ordinary discourse. It has nothing to do with the logical grammar of our ordinary color words. It is just a mistake to suppose that as the word "red" is actually used, it is ever surfaces in the sense of two-dimensional particulars which are red. The only particular involved when a physical object is "red on the outside, but green inside" is the physical object itself, located in a certain region of Space and enduring over a stretch of Time. The fundamental grammar of the attribute *red* is *physical object x is red at place p and at time t*. Certainly, when we say of an object that it is red, we commit ourselves to no more than that it is red "at the surface." And sometimes it is red at the surface by having what we would not hesitate to call a "part" which is red through and through—thus, a red table which is red by virtue of a layer of red paint. But the red paint is not itself red by virtue of a component—a 'surface' or 'expanse'; a particular with no thickness—which is red. There may, let me repeat, turn out to be some place in the total philosophical picture for the statement that there "really are" such particulars, and that they are elements in perceptual experience. But this place is not to be found by an analysis of ordinary perceptual discourse, any more than Minkowski four-dimensional Space-Time worms are an *analysis* of what we mean when we speak of physical objects in Space and Time.

## V. Impressions and Ideas: A Logical Point

**24.** Let me return to beating the neighboring bushes. Notice that the common descriptive component of the three experiences I am considering is itself often referred to (by philosophers, at least) as an *experience*—as, for example, an *immediate experience*. Here caution is necessary. The notorious "ing-ed" ambiguity of "experience" must be kept in mind. For although *seeing that x, over there, is red* is an *experiencing*—indeed, a paradigm case of experiencing—it does not follow that the descriptive content of this experiencing is itself an experiencing. Furthermore, because the fact that *x, over there, looks to Jones to be red* would be a *seeing*, on Jones' part, *that x, over there, is red*, if its propositional content were true, and because if it *were* a seeing, it *would be* an experiencing, we must beware of concluding that the fact that *x, over there, looks red to Jones* is itself an *experiencing*. Certainly, the fact that something looks red to me can itself be *experienced*. But it is not itself an experiencing.

All this is not to say that the common descriptive core may not turn out to be an experien*cing*, though the chances that this is so appear less with each step in my argument. On the other hand, I can say that it is a component in states of affairs which are experien*ced*, and it does not seem unreasonable to say that it is itself experien*ced*. But what kind of experience (in the sense of experien*ced*) *is* it? If my argument to date is sound, I cannot say that it is a *red* experience, that is, a red experienced item. I could, of course, introduce a new use of "red" according to which to say of an 'immediate experience' that it was red, would be the stipulated equivalent of characterizing it as that which could be the common descriptive component of a *seeing* that something is red, and the corresponding qualitative and existential *lookings*. This would give us a *predicate* by which to describe and report the experience, but we should, of course, be only verbally better off than if we could only refer to this kind of experience as *the kind which* could be the common descriptive component of a *seeing* and a qualitative or existential *looking*. And this makes it clear that one way of putting what we are after is by saying that we want to have a *name* for this kind of experience which is truly a *name*, and not just shorthand for a definite description. Does ordinary usage have a *name* for this kind of experience?

I shall return to this quest in a moment. In the meantime it is important to clear the way of a traditional obstacle to understanding the status of such things as *sensations of red triangles*. Thus, suppose I were to say that while the experience I am examining is not a red experience, it is an experience *of red*. I could expect the immediate challenge: "Is 'sensation of a red triangle' any better off than 'red and triangular experience'? Does not the existence of a sensation of a red triangle entail the existence of a red and triangular item, and hence, *always on the assumption that red is a property of physical objects*, of a red and triangular physical object? Must you not, therefore abandon this assumption, and return to the framework of sense contents which you have so far refused to do?"

One way out of dilemma would be to assimilate "Jones has a sensation of a red triangle" to "Jones believes in a divine Huntress." For the truth of the latter does not, of course, entail the existence of a divine Huntress. Now, I think that most contemporary philosophers are clear that it is possible to attribute to the context

. . . sensation of . . .

the *logical* property of being such that "There is a sensation of a red triangle" does not entail "There is a red triangle" without assimilating the context ". . . sensation of . . ." to the context ". . . believes in . . ." in any closer way. For while mentalistic verbs characteristically provide nonextensional contexts (when they are not "achievement" or "endorsing" words), not all nonextensional contexts are mentalistic. Thus, as far as the purely *logical* point is concerned, there is no reason why "Jones has a sensation of a red triangle" should be assimilated to "Jones believes in a divine Huntress" rather than to "It is possible that the moon is made of green cheese" or to any of the other nonextensional contexts familiar to logicians. Indeed there is no reason why it should be assimilated to any of these. ". . . sensation of . . ." or ". . . impression of . . ." could be a context which, though sharing with these others the logical property of nonextensionality, was otherwise in a class by itself.

**25.** Yet there is no doubt but that *historically* the contexts ". . . sensation of . . ." and ". . . impression of . . ." *were* assimilated to such mentalistic contexts as ". . . believes . . . ," ". . . desires . . . ," ". . . chooses . . . ," in short to contexts which are either themselves 'propositional attitudes' or involve propositional attitudes in their analysis. This assimilation took the form of classifying sensations with *ideas* or *thoughts*. Thus Descartes uses the word "thought" to cover not only *judgments, inferences, desires, volitions*, and (occurrent) *ideas of abstract qualities*, but also *sensations, feelings*, and *images*. Locke, in the same spirit, uses the term "idea" with similar scope. The apparatus of Conceptualism, which had its genesis in the controversy over universals, was given a correspondingly wide application. Just as objects and situations were said to have 'objective being' in our *thoughts*, when we think of them, or judge them to obtain—as contrasted with the 'subjective' or 'formal being' which they have in the world—so, when we have a sensation of a red triangle, the red triangle was supposed to have 'objective being' in our sensation.

In elaborating, for a moment, this conceptualistic interpretation of sensation, let me refer to that which has 'objective being' in a *thought* or *idea* as its *content* or *immanent object*. Then I can say that the fundamental difference between occurrent *abstract ideas* and *sensations,* for both Locke and Descartes, lay in the *specificity* and, above all, the *complexity* of the content of the latter. (Indeed, both Descartes and Locke assimilated the contrast between the simple and the complex in ideas to that between the generic and the specific.) Descartes thinks of sensations as confused thoughts of their external cause; Spinoza of sensations and images as confused thoughts of bodily states, and still more confused thoughts of the external causes of these bodily states. And it is interesting to note that the conceptualistic thesis that abstract entities have only *esse intentionale* (their *esse* is *concipi*) is extended by Descartes and, with less awareness of what he is doing, Locke, to include the thesis that colors, sounds, etc., exist "only in the mind" (their *esse* is *percipi*) and by Berkeley to cover all perceptible qualities.

Now, I think we would all agree, today, that this assimilation of sensations to thoughts is a mistake. It is sufficient to note that if "sensation of a red triangle" had the sense of "episode of the kind which is the common descriptive component of those experiences which *would be* cases of seeing that the facing surface of a physical object is red and triangular if an object *were* presenting a red and triangular facing surface" then it would have the nonextensionality the noticing of which led to this mistaken assimilation. But while we have indeed escaped from this blind alley, it is small consolation. For we are no further along in the search for a 'direct' or 'intrinsic' characterization of 'immediate experience.'

## VI. Impressions and Ideas: A Historical Point

**26.** There are those who will say that although I have spoken of exploring blind alleys, it is really I who am blind. For, they will say, if that which we wish to characterize intrinsically is an *experience*, then there *can* be no puzzle about knowing *what kind* of experience it is, though there may be a problem about how this knowledge is to be communicated to others. And, indeed, it is tempting to suppose that if we *should* happen, at a certain stage of our intellectual development, to be able to classify an experience *only* as *of the kind which* could be common to a *seeing* and corresponding qualitative and existential *lookings*, all we would have to do to acquire a 'direct designation' for this kind of experience would be to pitch in, 'examine' it, locate the kind which it exemplifies and which satisfies the above description, name it—say "φ"—and, in full possession of the concept of φ, classify such experiences, from now on, as φ experiences.

At this point, it is clear, the concept—or, as I have put it, the myth—of the given is being invoked to explain the possibility of a direct account of immediate experience. The myth insists that what I have been treating as one problem really subdivides into two, one of which is really no problem at all, while the other may have no solution. These problems are, respectively

(1) How do we become aware of an immediate experience as of one sort, and of a simultaneous immediate experience as of another sort?

(2) How can I know that the labels I attach to the sorts to which my immediate experiences belong, are attached by you to the same sorts? May not the sort I call "red" be the sort you call "green"—and so on systematically throughout the spectrum?

We shall find that the second question, to be a philosophical perplexity, presupposes a certain answer to the first question—indeed the answer given by the myth. And it is to this first question that I now turn. Actually there are various forms taken by the myth of the given in this connection, depending on other philosophical commitments. but they all have in common the idea that the awareness of certain *sorts* — and by "sorts" I have in mind, in the first instance, determinate sense repeatables — is a primordial, non-problematic feature of 'immediate experience.' In the context of conceptualism, as we have seen, this idea took the form of treating sensations as though they were absolutely specific, and infinitely complicated, *thoughts*. And it is essential to an understanding of the empiricist tradition to realize that whereas the contemporary problem of universals primarily concerns the status of repeatable *determinate* features of particular situations, and the contemporary problem of abstract ideas is at least as much the problem of what it is to be aware of determinate repeatables as of what it is to be aware of determinable repeatables, Locke, Berkeley and, for that matter, Hume saw the problem of abstract ideas as the problem of what it is to be aware of *determinable* repeatables.* Thus, an examination of Locke's *Essay* makes it clear that he is thinking of a sensation of white as the sort of thing that can become an abstract idea (occurrent) of White — a thought of White "in the Understanding" — merely by virtue of being separated from the context of other sensations (and images) which accompany it on a particular occasion. In other words, for Locke an abstract (occurrent) idea of the determinate repeatable Whiteness is nothing more than an isolated *image of white*, which, in turn, differs from a *sensation of white* only (to use a modern turn of phrase) by being "centrally aroused."

* For a systematic elaboration and defence of the following interpretation of Locke, Berkeley, and Hume, the reader should consult (11).

In short, for Locke, the problem of how we come to be aware of *determinate* sense repeatables is no problem at all. Merely by virtue of having sensations and images we have this awareness. *His* problem of abstract ideas is the problem of how we come to be able to think of generic properties. And, as is clear from the *Essay*, he approaches *this* problem in terms of what might be called an "adjunctive theory of specification," that is, the view that (if we represent the idea of a determinable as *the idea of being A*) the idea of a determinate form of A can be represented *as the idea of being A and B*. It is, of course, notorious that this won't account for the relation of *the idea of being red* to *the idea of being crimson*. By thinking of *conjunction* as the fundamental logical relation involved in building up complex ideas from simple ones, and as the principle of the difference between determinable and determinate ideas, Locke precluded himself from giving even a plausible account of the relation between ideas of determinables and ideas of determinates. It is interesting to speculate what turn his thought might have taken had he admitted *disjunctive* as well as *conjunctive* complex ideas, *the idea of being A or B* alongside *the idea of being A and B*.

**27.** But my purpose here is not to develop a commentary on the shortcomings of Locke's treatment of abstract ideas, but to emphasize that something which is a problem for us was not a problem for him. And it is therefore important to note that the same is true of Berkeley. His problem was not, as it is often construed, "How do we go from the awareness of *particulars* to ideas of *repeatables*?" but rather "Granted that in immediate experience we are aware of absolutely *specific* sense qualities, how do we come to be conscious of genera pertaining to them, and in what does this consciousness consist?" (This is not the only dimension of "abstraction" that concerned him, but it is the one that is central to our purpose.) And, contrary to the usual interpretation, the essential difference between his account and Locke's consists in the fact that whereas Locke was on the whole* committed to the view that there can be an idea which is *of* the genus without being *of* any of its species, Berkeley insists that we can have an idea *of* a genus only by having an idea *of* the genus *as*, to borrow a useful Scotist term, *'contracted' into one of its species.*

Roughly, Berkeley's contention is that if *being A* entails *being B*, then there can be no such thing as an idea which is *of A* without being *of B*. He infers that since *being triangular* entails *having some determinately triangular shape*, there cannot be an idea which is *of triangle* without being *of some determinately triangular shape*. We can be aware of generic triangularity only by having an idea which is of triangularity as 'contracted' into one of the specific forms of triangularity. Any of the latter will do; they are all "of the same sort."

* I say that Locke was "on the whole" committed to the view that there can be an idea which is *of* the genus without being *of* any of its species, because while he saw that it couldn't be *of* any one of the species to the exclusion of the others, and saw no way of avoiding this except by making it *of none* of the species, he was greatly puzzled by this, for he saw that in some sense the idea *of the genus* must be *of all the species*. We have already noted that if he had admitted disjunction as a principle of compounding ideas, he could have said that the idea *of the genus* is the idea *of the disjunction of all its species*, that the idea of *being triangular* is the idea of *being scalene or isosceles*. As it was, he thought that to be of all the species it would have to be the idea of *being scalene and isosceles*, which is, of course, the idea of an impossibility.

It is interesting to note that if Berkeley had faced up to the implications of the criterion we shall find him to have adopted, this disjunctive conception of the generic idea is the one he would have been led to adopt. For since *being G*—where 'G' stands for a generic character—entails being $S_1$ or $S_2$ or $S_3$ . . . . . or $S_n$,—where '$S_1$' stands for a specific character falling under G—Berkeley should have taken as the unit of ideas concerning triangles, the idea of the genus Triangle as differentiated into the set of specific forms of triangularity. But, needless to say, if Berkeley *had* taken this step, he could not have thought of a sensation of crimson as a determinate *thought*.

**28.** Now, a careful study of the *Treatise* makes it clear that Hume is in the same boat as Berkeley and Locke, sharing with them the presupposition that we have an unacquired ability to be aware of determinate repeatables. It is often said that whereas he begins the *Treatise* by characterizing 'ideas' in terms which do not distinguish between *images* and *thoughts*, he corrects this deficiency in Book I, Part I, Section vii. What these students of Hume tend to overlook is that what Hume does in this later section is give an account *not* of what it is to think of *repeatables* whether determinable or determinate, but of what it is to think of *determinables*, thus of color as contrasted with particular shades of color. And his account of the consciousness of determinables takes for granted that we have a primordial ability to take account of *determinate* repeatables. Thus, his later account is simply built on, and in no sense a revision of, the account of ideas with which he opens the *Treatise*.

How, then, does he differ from Berkeley and Locke? The latter two had supposed that there must be such a thing as an *occurrent* thought of a determinable, however much they differed in their account of such thoughts. Hume, on the other hand, assuming that there are occurrent thoughts of *determinate* repeatables, *denies* that there are occurrent thoughts of *determinables*. I shall spare the reader the familiar details of Hume's attempt to give a constructive account of our consciousness of determinables, nor shall I criticize it. For my point is that however much Locke, Berkeley, and Hume differ on the problem of abstract ideas, they all take for granted that the human mind has an innate ability to be aware of certain determinate sorts — *indeed, that we are aware of them simply by virtue of having sensations and images.*

**29.** Now, it takes but a small twist of Hume's position to get a radically different view. For suppose that instead of characterizing the initial elements of experience as impressions of, *e.g. red*, Hume had characterized them *as red particulars* (and I would be the last to deny that not only Hume, but perhaps Berkeley and Locke as well, often treat impressions or ideas *of red* as though they were *red particulars*) then Hume's view, expanded to take into account determinates as well as determinables, would become the view that all consciousness of sorts or repeatables rests on an association of *words* (e.g. "red") with classes of resembling particulars.

It clearly makes all the difference in the world how this association is conceived. For if the formation of the association involves not only the occurrence of resembling particulars, but also the occurrence of the awareness *that they are resembling particulars*, then the givenness of determinate kinds or repeatables, say crimson, is merely being replaced by the givenness of *facts* of the form *x resembles y*, and we are back with an unacquired ability to be aware of repeatables, in this case the repeatable *resemblance*. Even more obviously, if the formation of the association involves not only the occurrence of red particulars, but the awareness *that they are red*, then the conceptualistic form of the myth has merely been replaced by a realistic version, as in the classical sense-datum theory.

If, however, the association is not mediated by the awareness of facts either of the form *x resembles y*, or of the form *x is ϕ*, then we have a view of the general type which I will call *psychological nominalism*, according to which *all* awareness of *sorts, resemblances, facts*, etc., in short, all awareness of abstract entities—indeed, all awareness even of particulars—is a linguistic affair. According to it, not even the awareness of such sorts, resemblances, and facts as pertain to so-called immediate experience is presupposed by the process of acquiring the use of a language.

Two remarks are immediately relevant: (1) Although the

form of psychological nominalism which one gets by modi-
fying Hume's view along the above lines has the essential
merit that it avoids the mistake of supposing that there are
pure episodes of being aware of sensory repeatables or sensory facts, and is committed to the view that any event which
can be referred to in these terms must be, to use Ryle's
expression, a mongrel categorical-hypothetical, in particular,
a verbal episode *as being the manifestation of associative connections of the word-object and word-word types*, it nevertheless is
impossibly crude and inadequate as an account of the simplest concept. (2) Once sensations and images have been
purged of epistemic aboutness, the primary reason for supposing that the fundamental associative tie between language
and the world must be between words and 'immediate experiences' has disappeared, and the way is clear to recognizing
that basic word-world associations hold, for example, between "red" and red *physical objects*, rather than between "red"
and a supposed class of private red particulars.

The second remark, it should be emphasized, does not
imply that private sensations or impressions may not be
essential to the formation of these associative connections.
For one can certainly admit that the tie between "red" and
red physical objects—which tie makes it possible for "red"
to mean the quality red—is *causally* mediated by sensations
of red without being committed to the mistaken idea that it
is "really" sensations of red, rather than red physical objects,
which are the primary denotation of the word "red."

## VII. The Logic of 'Means'

**30.** There is a source of the Myth of the Given to which even
philosophers who are suspicious of the whole idea of *inner
episodes* can fall prey. This is the fact that when we picture a

child—or a carrier of slabs—learning his *first* language, *we*, of course, locate the language learner in a structured logical space in which we are at home. Thus, we conceive of him as a person (or, at least, a potential person) in a world of physical objects, colored, producing sounds, existing in Space and Time. But though it is *we* who are familiar with this logical space, we run the danger, if we are not careful, of picturing the language learner as having *ab initio* some degree of awareness—"pre-analytic," limited and fragmentary though it may be—of this same logical space. We picture his state as though it were rather like our own when placed in a strange forest on a dark night. In other words, unless we are careful, we can easily take for granted that the process of teaching a child to use a language is that of teaching it to discriminate elements within a logical space of particulars, universals, facts, etc., of which it is already undiscriminatingly aware, and to associate these discriminated elements with verbal symbols. And this mistake is in principle the same whether the logical space of which the child is supposed to have this undiscriminating awareness is conceived by *us* to be that of physical objects or of private sense contents.

The real test of a theory of language lies not in its account of what has been called (by H. H. Price) "thinking in absence," but in its account of "thinking in presence"—that is to say, its account of those occasions on which the fundamental connection of language with nonlinguistic fact is exhibited. And many theories which look like psychological nominalism when one views their account of thinking in absence, turn out to be quite "Augustinian" when the scalpel is turned to their account of thinking in presence.

**31.** Now, the friendly use I have been making of the phrase "psychological nominalism" may suggest that I am about to *equate* concepts with words, and thinking, in so far as it is episodic, with verbal episodes. I must now hasten to say that I shall do nothing of the sort, or, at least, that if I *do* do *something* of the sort, the view I shall shortly be developing is only in a relatively Pickwickian sense an equation of thinking with the use of language. I wish to emphasize, therefore, that as I am using the term, the primary connotation of "psychological nominalism" is the denial that there is any awareness of logical space prior to, or independent of, the acquisition of a language.

However, although I shall later be distinguishing between *thoughts* and their verbal *expression*, there is a point of fundamental importance which is best made before more subtle distinctions are drawn. To begin with, it is perfectly clear that the word "red" would not be a *predicate* if it didn't have the logical syntax characteristic of predicates. Nor would it be the predicate it is, unless, in certain frames of mind, at least, we tended to respond to red objects in standard circumstances with something having the force of "This is red." And once we have abandoned the idea that learning to use the word "red" involves antecedent episodes of the *awareness of redness*—not to be confused, of course, with *sensations of red*—there is a temptation to suppose that the word "red" means the quality *red* by virtue of these two facts: briefly, the fact that it has the *syntax* of a predicate, and the fact that it is a *response* (in certain circumstances) to red objects.

But this account of the meaningfulness of "red," which Price has correctly stigmatized as the "thermometer view," would have little plausibility if it were not reinforced by another line of thought which takes its point of departure from the superficial resemblance of

(In German) *"rot"* means *red*

to such relational statements as

Cowley adjoins Oxford.

For once one assimilates the form

". . ." means - - -

to the form                         x R y

and thus takes it for granted that meaning is a relation between a word and a nonverbal entity, it is tempting to suppose that the relation in question is that of association.

The truth of the matter, of course, is that statements of the form "'. . .' means - - -" are *not* relational statements, and that while it is indeed the case that the word *"rot"* could not mean the quality *red* unless it were associated with red things, it would be misleading to say that the semantical statement *"'Rot'* means *red"* says of *"rot"* that it associated with red things. For this would suggest that the semantical statement is, so to speak, definitional shorthand for a longer statement about the associative connections of *"rot,"* which is not the case. The rubric "'. . .' means - - -" is a linguistic device for conveying the information that a *mentioned* word, in this case *"rot,"* plays the same role in a certain linguistic economy, in this case the linguistic economy of German-speaking peoples, as does the word "red," which is not *mentioned* but *used*—used in a unique way; *exhibited,* so to speak—and which occurs "on the right-hand side" of the semantical statement.

We see, therefore, how the two statements

*"Und"* means *and*

and

*"Rot"* means *red*

can tell us quite different things about *"und"* and *"rot,"* for the first conveys the information that *"und"* plays the purely formal role of a certain logical connective, the second that *"rot"* plays in German the role of the observation word "red"—in spite of the fact that *means* has the same sense in each statement, and without having to say that the first says of *"und"* that it stands in "the meaning relation" to Conjunction, or the second that *"rot"* stands in "the meaning relation" to Redness.*

These considerations make it clear that nothing whatever can be inferred about the complexity of the role played by the word "red" or about the exact way in which the word "red" is related to red things, from the truth of the semantical statement "'red' means the quality *red*." And no consideration arising from the 'Fido'-Fido aspect of the grammar of "means" precludes one from claiming that the role of the word "red" by virtue of which it can correctly be said to have the meaning it does is a complicated one indeed, and that one cannot understand the meaning of the word "red"— "know what redness is"—unless one has a great deal of knowledge which classical empiricism would have held to have a purely contingent relationship with the possession of fundamental empirical concepts.

## VIII. Does Empirical Knowledge Have a Foundation?

**32.** One of the forms taken by the Myth of the Given is the idea that there is, indeed *must be,* a structure of particular matter of fact such that (a) each fact can not only be noninferentially known to be the case, but presupposes no other

---

* For an analysis of the problem of abstract entities built on this interpretation of semantical statements, see (20).

knowledge either of particular matter of fact, or of general truths; and (b) such that the noninferential knowledge of facts belonging to this structure constitutes the ultimate court of appeals for all factual claims—particular and general—about the world. It is important to note that I characterized the knowledge of fact belonging to this stratum as not only noninferential, but as pre-supposing no knowledge of other matter of fact, whether particular or general. It might be thought that this is a redundancy, that knowledge (not belief or conviction, but knowledge) which logically presupposes knowledge of other facts *must* be inferential. This, however, as I hope to show, is itself an episode in the Myth.

Now, the idea of such a privileged stratum of fact is a familiar one, though not without its difficulties. Knowledge pertaining to this level is *noninferential,* yet it is, after all, *knowledge.* It is *ultimate,* yet it has *authority.* The attempt to make a consistent picture of these two requirements has traditionally taken the following form:

Statements pertaining to this level, in order to 'express knowledge' must not only be made, but, so to speak, must be worthy of being made, *credible,* that is, in the sense of worthy of credence. Furthermore, and this is a crucial point, they must be made in a way which *involves* this credibility. For where there is no connection between the making of a statement and its authority, the assertion may express *conviction,* but it can scarcely be said to express knowledge.

The authority—the credibility—of statements pertaining to this level cannot exhaustively consist in the fact that they are supported by *other* statements, for in that case all *knowledge* pertaining to this level would have to be inferential, which not only contradicts the hypothesis, but flies in the face of good sense. The conclusion seems inevitable that if some statements pertaining to this level are to express *noninferential* knowledge, they must have a credibility which is not a matter of being supported by other statements. Now there does seem to be a class of statements which fill at least part of this bill, namely such statements as would be said to *report observations,* thus, "This is red." These statements, candidly made, have authority. Yet they are not expressions of inference. How, then, is this authority to be understood?

Clearly, the argument continues, it springs from the fact that they are made in just the circumstances in which they are made, as is indicated by the fact that they characteristically, though not necessarily or without exception, involve those so-called token-reflexive expressions which, in addition to the tenses of verbs, serve to connect the circumstances in which a statement is made with its sense. (At this point it will be helpful to begin putting the line of thought I am developing in terms of the *fact-stating* and *observation-reporting* roles of certain sentences.) Roughly, two verbal performances which are tokens of a non-token-reflexive sentence can occur in widely different circumstances and yet make the same statement; whereas two tokens of a token-reflexive sentence can make the same statement only if they are uttered in the same circumstances (according to a relevant criterion of sameness). And two tokens of a sentence, whether it contains a token-reflexive expression—over and above a tensed verb—or not, can make the same *report* only if, made in all candor, they express the *presence*—in *some* sense of "presence"—of the state of affairs that is being reported; if, that is, they stand in that relation to the state of affairs, whatever the relation may be, by virtue of which they can be said to formulate observations of it.

It would appear, then, that there are two ways in which a sentence token can have credibility: (1) The authority may accrue to it, so to speak, from above, that is, as being a token of a sentence type *all* the tokens of which, in a certain use, have credibility, e.g. "2 + 2 = 4." In this case, let us say that token credibility is inherited from type authority. (2) The credibility may accrue to it from the fact that it came to exist in a certain way in a certain set of circumstances, e.g. "This is red." Here token credibility is not derived from type credibility.

Now, the credibility of *some* sentence types appears to be *intrinsic*—at least in the limited sense that it is *not* derived from other sentences, type or token. This is, or seems to be, the case with certain sentences used to make analytic statements. The credibility of *some* sentence types accrues to them by virtue of their logical relations to other sentence types, thus by virtue of the fact that they are logical consequences of more basic sentences. It would seem obvious, however, that the credibility of empirical sentence types cannot be traced without remainder to the credibility of other sentence types. And since no empirical sentence type appears to have *intrinsic* credibility, this means that credibility must accrue to *some* empirical sentence types by virtue of their logical relations to certain sentence tokens, and, indeed, to sentence tokens the authority of which is not derived, in its turn, from the authority of sentence types.

The picture we get is that of their being two *ultimate* modes of credibility: (1) The intrinsic credibility of analytic sentences, which accrues to tokens as being tokens of such a type; (2) the credibility of such tokens as "express observations," a credibility which flows from tokens to types.

**33.** Let us explore this picture, which is common to all traditional empiricisms, a bit further. How is the authority of such sentence tokens as "express observational knowledge" to be understood? It has been tempting to suppose that in spite of the obvious differences which exist between "observation reports" and "analytic statements," there is an essential similarity between the ways in which they come by their authority. Thus, it has been claimed, not without plausibility, that whereas *ordinary* empirical statements can be *correctly* made without being *true*, observation reports resemble analytic statements in that being correctly made is a sufficient as well as necessary condition of their truth. And it has been inferred from this—somewhat hastily, I believe—that "correctly making" the report "This is green" is a matter of "following the rules for the use of 'this,' 'is' and 'green.'"

Three comments are immediately necessary:

(1) First a brief remark about the term "report." In ordinary usage a report is a report made *by* someone *to* someone. To make a report is to *do* something. In the literature of epistemology, however, the word "report" or "*Konstatierung*" has acquired a technical use in which a sentence token can play a reporting role (a) without being an *overt* verbal performance, and (b) without having the character of being "by someone to someone"—even oneself. There is, of course, such a thing as "talking to oneself"—*in foro interno*—but, as I shall be emphasizing in the closing stages of my argument, it is important not to suppose that all "covert" verbal episodes are of this kind.

(2) My second comment is that while *we* shall not assume that because 'reports' *in the ordinary sense* are *actions*, 'reports' in the sense of *Konstatierungen* are also actions, the line of thought we are considering treats them as such. In other words, it interprets the correctness of *Konstatierungen* as analogous to the rightness of actions. Let me emphasize, however, that not all *ought* is *ought to do*, nor all correctness the correctness of *actions*.

(3) My third comment is that if the expression "following

a rule" is taken seriously, and is not weakened beyond all recognition into the bare notion of exhibiting a uniformity — in which case the lightning, thunder sequence would "follow a rule"—then it is the knowledge or belief that the circumstances are of a certain kind, and not the mere fact that they *are* of this kind, which contributes to bringing about the action.

**34.** In the light of these remarks it is clear that *if* observation reports are construed as *actions*, *if* their correctness is interpreted as the correctness of an *action,* and *if* the authority of an observation report is construed as the fact that making it is "following a rule" in the proper sense of this phrase, *then* we are face to face with givenness in its most straightforward form. For these stipulations commit one to the idea that the authority of *Konstatierungen* rests on nonverbal episodes of awareness—awareness *that* something is the case, e.g. *that this is green*—which nonverbal episodes have an intrinsic authority (they are, so to speak 'self-authenticating') which the *verbal* performances (the *Konstatierungen*) properly performed "express." One is committed to a stratum of authoritative nonverbal episodes ("awareness") the authority of which accrues to a superstructure of *verbal actions*, provided that the expressions occurring in these actions are properly *used*. These self-authenticating episodes would constitute the tortoise on which stands the elephant on which rests the edifice of empirical knowledge. The essence of the view is the same whether these intrinsically authoritative episodes are such items as the awareness that a certain sense content is green or such items as the awareness that a certain physical object looks to someone to be green.

**35.** But what is the alternative? We might begin by trying something like the following: An overt or covert token of

"This is green" in the presence of a green item is a *Konsta-tierung* and expresses observational knowledge if and only if it is a manifestation of a tendency to produce overt or covert tokens of "This is green"—given a certain set—if and only if a green object is being looked at in standard conditions. Clearly on this interpretation the occurrence of such tokens of "This is green" would be "following a rule" only in the sense that they are instances of a uniformity, a uniformity differing from the lightning-thunder case in that it is an acquired causal characteristic of the language user. Clearly the above suggestion, which corresponds to the "thermome-ter view" criticized by Professor Price, and which we have already rejected, won't do as it stands. Let us see, however, if it can't be revised to fit the criteria I have been using for "expressing observational knowledge."

The first hurdle to be jumped concerns the *authority* which, as I have emphasized, a sentence token must have in order that it may be said to express knowledge. Clearly, on this account the only thing that can remotely be supposed to constitute such authority is the fact that one can infer the presence of a green object from the fact that someone makes this report. As we have already noticed, the correctness of a report does not have to be construed as the rightness of an *action*. A report can be correct as being an instance of a general mode of behavior which, in a given linguistic com-munity, it is reasonable to sanction and support.

The second hurdle is, however, the decisive one. For we have seen that to be the expression of knowledge, a report must not only *have* authority, this authority must *in some sense* be recognized by the person whose report it is. And this is a steep hurdle indeed. For if the authority of the report "This is green" lies in the fact that the existence of green items appropriately related to the perceiver can be inferred from the occurrence of such reports, it follows that only a person who is able to draw this inference, and therefore who has not only the concept *green,* but also the concept of uttering "This is green"—indeed, the concept of certain conditions of perception, those which would correctly be called 'standard conditions'—could be in a position to token "This is green" in recognition of its authority. In other words, for a *Konstatierung* "This is green" to "express observational knowledge," not only must it be a *symptom* or *sign* of the presence of a green object in standard conditions, but the perceiver must know that tokens of "This is green" *are* symptoms of the presence of green objects in conditions which are standard for visual perception.

**36.** Now it might be thought that there is something obviously absurd in the idea that before a token uttered by, say, Jones could be the expression of observational knowledge, Jones would have to know that overt verbal episodes of this kind are reliable indicators of the existence, suitably related to the speaker, of green objects. I do not think that it is. Indeed, I think that something very like it is true. The point I wish to make now, however, is that if it *is* true, then it follows, as a matter of simple logic, that one couldn't have observational knowledge of *any* fact unless one knew many *other* things as well. And let me emphasize that the point is not taken care of by distinguishing between *knowing how* and *knowing that,* and admitting that observational knowledge requires a lot of "know how." For the point is specifically that observational knowledge of any particular fact, e.g. that this is green, presupposes that one knows general facts of the form *X is a reliable symptom of Y.* And to admit this requires an abandonment of the traditional empiricist idea that observational knowledge "stands on its own feet." Indeed, the suggestion would be anathema to traditional empiricists for the obvious reason that by making observational knowledge *presuppose* knowledge of general facts of the form *X is a reliable symptom of Y*, it runs counter to the idea that we come to know general facts of this form only *after* we have come to know by observation a number of particular facts which support the hypothesis that X is a symptom of Y.

And it might be thought that there is an obvious regress in the view we are examining. Does it not tell us that observational knowledge at time t presupposes knowledge of the form *X is a reliable symptom of Y*, which presupposes *prior* observational knowledge, which presupposes *other* knowledge of the form *X is a reliable symptom of Y*, which presupposes still other, and *prior,* observational knowledge, and so on? This charge, however, rests on too simple, indeed a radically mistaken, conception of what one is saying of Jones when one says that he *knows* that p. It is not just that the objection supposes that knowing is an *episode;* for clearly there are episodes which we can correctly characterize as knowings, in particular, *observings.* The essential point is that in characterizing an episode or a state as that of *knowing,* we are not giving an empirical description of that episode or state; we are placing it in the logical space of reasons, of justifying and being able to justify what one says.

**37.** Thus, all that the view I am defending requires is that no tokening by S *now* of "This is green" is to count as "expressing observational knowledge" unless it is also correct to say of S that he *now* knows the appropriate fact of the form *X is a reliable symptom of Y,* namely that (and again I oversimplify) utterances of "This is green" are reliable indicators of the presence of green objects in standard conditions of perception. And while the correctness of this statement about Jones requires that Jones could *now* cite prior particular facts as evidence for the idea that these utterances *are* reliable indicators, it requires only that it is correct to say that Jones *now* knows, thus remembers, that these particular facts *did* obtain. It does not require that it be correct to say that at the time these facts did obtain he *then knew* them to obtain. And the regress disappears.

Thus, while Jones' ability to give inductive reasons *today* is built on a long history of acquiring and manifesting verbal habits in perceptual situations, and, in particular, the occurrence of verbal episodes, e.g. "This is green," which is superficially like those which are later properly said to express observational knowledge, it does not require that any episode in this prior time be characterizeable as expressing knowledge. (At this point, the reader should reread Section 19 above.)

**38.** The idea that observation "strictly and properly so-called" is constituted by certain self-authenticating nonverbal episodes, the authority of which is transmitted to verbal and quasi-verbal performances when these performances are made "in conformity with the semantical rules of the language," is, of course, the heart of the Myth of the Given. For the *given*, in epistemological tradition, is what is *taken* by these self-authenticating episodes. These 'takings' are, so to speak, the unmoved movers of empirical knowledge, the 'knowings in presence' which are presupposed by all other knowledge, both the knowledge of general truths and the knowledge 'in absence' of other particular matters of fact. Such is the framework in which traditional empiricism makes its characteristic claim that the perceptually given is the foundation of empirical knowledge.

Let me make it clear, however, that if I reject this framework, it is not because I should deny that observings are *inner* episodes, nor that *strictly speaking* they are *nonverbal* episodes. It will be my contention, however, that the sense in which they are nonverbal—which is also the sense in which thought episodes are nonverbal—is one which gives no aid or comfort to epistemological givenness. In the concluding sections of this paper, I shall attempt to explicate the logic of inner episodes, and show that we can distinguish between observations and thoughts, on the one hand, and their verbal expression on the other, without making the mistakes of traditional dualism. I shall also attempt to explicate the logical status of *impressions* or *immediate experiences*, and thus bring to a successful conclusion the quest with which my argument began.

One final remark before I begin this task. If I reject the framework of traditional empiricism, it is not because I want to say that empirical knowledge has *no* foundation. For to put it this way is to suggest that it is really "empirical knowledge so-called," and to put it in a box with rumors and hoaxes. There is clearly *some* point to the picture of human knowledge as resting on a level of propositions—observation reports—which do not rest on other propositions in the same way as other propositions rest on them. On the other hand, I do wish to insist that the metaphor of "foundation" is misleading in that it keeps us from seeing that if there is a logical dimension in which other empirical propositions rest on observation reports, there is another logical dimension in which the latter rest on the former.

*Above all*, the picture is misleading because of its static character. One seems forced to choose between the picture of an elephant which rests on a tortoise (What supports the tortoise?) and the picture of a great Hegelian serpent of knowledge with its tail in its mouth (Where does it begin?). Neither will do. For empirical knowledge, like its sophisticated extension, science, is rational, not because it has a *foundation* but because it is a self-correcting enterprise which can put *any* claim in jeopardy, though not *all* at once.

## IX. Science and Ordinary Usage

**39.** There are many strange and exotic specimens in the gardens of philosophy: Epistemology, Ontology, Cosmology, to name but a few. And clearly there is much good sense — not only rhyme but reason — to these labels. It is not my purpose, however, to animadvert on the botanizing of philosophies and things philosophical, other than to call attention to a recent addition to the list of philosophical flora and fauna, the Philosophy of Science. Nor shall I attempt to locate this new specialty in a classificatory system. The point I wish to make, however, can be introduced by calling to mind the fact that classificatory schemes, however theoretical their purpose, have practical consequences: nominal causes, so to speak, have real effects. As long as there was no such subject as 'philosophy of science,' all students of philosophy felt obligated to keep at least one eye part of the time on both the methodological and the substantive aspects of the scientific enterprise. And if the result was often a confusion of the task of philosophy with the task of science, and almost equally often a projection of the framework of the latest scientific speculations into the common-sense picture of the world (witness the almost unquestioned assumption, today, that the common-sense world of physical objects in Space and Time must be *analyzable* into spatially and temporally, or even spatiotemporally, related *events*), at least it had the merit of ensuring that reflection on the nature and implications of scientific discourse was an integral and vital part of philosophical thinking generally. But now that philosophy of science has nominal as well as real existence, there has arisen the temptation to leave it to the specialists, and to confuse the sound idea that philosophy is not science with the mistaken idea that philosophy is independent of science.

**40.** As long as discourse was viewed as a map, subdivided into a side-by-side of sub-maps, each representing a subregion in a side-by-side of regions making up the total subject matter of discourse, and as long as the task of the philosopher was conceived to be the piecemeal one of analysis in the sense of *definition*—the task, so to speak, of "making little ones out of big ones"—one could view with equanimity the existence of philosophical specialists—specialists in formal and mathematical logic, in perception, in moral philosophy, etc. For if discourse were as represented above, where would be the harm of each man fencing himself off in his own garden? In spite, however, of the persistence of the slogan "philosophy is analysis," we now realize that the atomistic conception of philosophy is a snare and a delusion. For "analysis" no longer connotes the definition of terms, but rather the clarification of the logical structure—in the broadest sense—of discourse, and discourse no longer appears as one plane parallel to another, but as a tangle of intersecting dimensions whose relations with one another and with extra-linguistic fact conform to no single or simple pattern. No longer can the philosopher interested in perception say "let him who is interested in prescriptive discourse analyze its concepts and leave me in peace." Most if not all philosophically interesting concepts are caught up in more than one dimension of discourse, and while the atomism of early analysis has a healthy successor in the contemporary stress on journeyman tactics, the grand strategy of the philosophical enterprise is once again directed toward that articulated and integrated vision of man-in-the-universe — or, shall I say discourse-about-man-in-all-discourse — which has traditionally been its goal.

But the moral I wish specifically to draw is that no longer can one smugly say "Let the person who is interested in scientific discourse analyze scientific discourse and let the person who is interested in ordinary discourse analyze ordinary discourse." Let me not be misunderstood. I am not saying that in order to discern the logic — the polydimensional logic — of ordinary discourse, it is necessary to make use of the results or the methods of the sciences. Nor even that, within limits, such a division of labor is not a sound corollary of the journeyman's approach. My point is rather that what we call the scientific enterprise is the flowering of a dimension of discourse which already exists in what historians call the "prescientific stage," and that failure to understand this type of discourse "writ large" — in science — may lead, indeed, has often led to a failure to appreciate its role in "ordinary usage," and, as a result, to a failure to understand the full logic of even the most fundamental, the "simplest" empirical terms.

**41.** Another point of equal importance. The procedures of philosophical analysis as such may make no use of the methods or results of the sciences. But familiarity with the trend of scientific thought is essential to the *appraisal* of the framework categories of the common-sense picture of the world. For if the line of thought embodied in the preceding paragraphs is sound, if, that is to say, scientific discourse is but a continuation of a dimension of discourse which has been present in human discourse from the very beginning, then one would expect there to be a sense in which the scientific picture of the world *replaces* the common-sense picture; a sense in which the scientific account of "what there is" *supersedes* the descriptive ontology of everyday life.

Here one must be cautious. For there is a right way and a wrong way to make this point. Many years ago it used to be confidently said that science has shown, for example, that physical objects aren't really colored. Later it was pointed out that if this is interpreted as the claim that the sentence "Physical objects have colors" expresses an empirical proposition which, though widely believed by common sense, has been shown by science to be false, then, of course, this claim is absurd. The idea that physical objects aren't colored can make sense only as the (misleading) expression of one aspect of a philosophical critique of the very framework of physical objects located in Space and enduring through Time. In short, "Physical objects aren't really colored" makes sense only as a clumsy expression of the idea that there are no such things as the colored physical objects of the common-sense world, where this is interpreted, not as an empirical proposition—like "There are no nonhuman featherless bipeds"— *within* the common-sense frame, but as the expression of a rejection (in *some* sense) of this very framework itself, in favor of another built around different, if not unrelated, categories. This rejection need not, of course, be a *practical* rejection. It need not, that is, carry with it a proposal to brain-wash existing populations and train them to speak differently. And, of course, as long as the existing framework is used, it will be *incorrect* to say—otherwise than to make a philosophical point *about the framework*—that no object is really colored, or is located in Space, or endures through

Time. But, *speaking as a philosopher,* I am quite prepared to say that the common-sense world of physical objects in Space and Time is unreal—that is, that there are no such things. Or, to put it less paradoxically, that in the dimension of describing and explaining the world, science is the measure of all things, of what is that it is, and of what is not that it is not.

**43.** There is a widespread impression that reflection on how we learn the language in which, in everyday life, we describe the world, leads to the conclusion that the categories of the common-sense picture of the world have, so to speak, an unchallengeable authenticity. There are, of course, different conceptions of just what this fundamental categorial framework is. For some it is sense contents and phenomenal relations between them; for others physical objects, persons, and processes in Space and Time. But whatever their points of difference, the philosophers I have in mind are united in the conviction that what is called the "ostensive tie" between our fundamental descriptive vocabulary and the world rules out of court as utterly absurd any notion that there are no such things as this framework talks about.

An integral part of this conviction is what I shall call (in an extended sense) the *positivistic conception of science,* the idea that the framework of theoretical objects (molecules, electromagnetic fields, etc.) and their relationships is, so to speak, an *auxiliary* framework. In its most explicit form, it is the idea that theoretical objects and propositions concerning them are "calculational devices," the value and status of which consist in their systematizing and heuristic role with respect to confirmable generalizations formulated in the framework of terms which enjoy a direct ostensive link with the world. One is tempted to put this by saying that according to these philosophers, the objects of ostensively linked discourse behave as *if* and *only* as *if* they were bound up with or consisted of scientific entities. But, of course, these philosophers would hasten to point out (and rightly so) that

X behaves as if it consisted of Y's

makes sense only by contrast with

X behaves as it does because it *does* consist of Y's

whereas their contention is exactly that where the Y's are *scientific* objects, no such contrast makes sense.

The point I am making is that as long as one thinks that there is a framework, whether of physical objects or of sense contents, the absolute authenticity of which is guaranteed by the fact that the learning of this framework involves an "ostensive step," so long one will be tempted to think of the authority of theoretical discourse as entirely derivative, that of a calculational auxiliary, an effective heuristic device. It is one of my prime purposes, in the following sections, to convince the reader that this interpretation of the status of the scientific picture of the world rests on two mistakes: (1) a misunderstanding (which I have already exposed) of the ostensive element in the learning and use of a language—the Myth of the Given; (2) a reification of the *methodological* distinction between theoretical and non-theoretical discourse into a *substantive* distinction between theoretical and non-theoretical existence.

**44.** One way of summing up what I have been saying above is by saying that there is a widespread impression abroad, aided and abetted by a naive interpretation of concept formation, that philosophers of science deal with a mode of discourse which is, so to speak, a peninsular offshoot from the mainland of ordinary discourse. The study of scientific discourse is conceived to be a worthy employment for those who have the background and motivation to keep track of it, but an employment which is fundamentally a hobby divorced from the perplexities of the mainland. But, of course, this summing up won't quite do. For all philosophers would agree that no philosophy would be complete unless it resolved the perplexities which arise when one attempts to think through the relationship of the framework of modern science to ordinary discourse. My point, however, is not that any one would reject the idea that this is a proper task for philosophy, but that, by approaching the language in which the plain man describes and explains empirical fact with the presuppositions of *givenness,* they are led to a "resolution" of these perplexities along the lines of what I have called the positivistic or peninsular conception of scientific discourse— a "resolution" which, I believe, is not only superficial, but positively mistaken.

## X. Private Episodes: The Problem

**45.** Let us now return, after a long absence, to the problem of how the similarity among the experiences of *seeing that an object over there is red, its looking to one that an object over there is red* (when in point of fact it is *not* red) and *its looking to one as though there were a red object over there* (when in fact there is *nothing* over there at all) is to be understood. Part of this similarity, we saw, consists in the fact that they all involve the idea—the proposition, if you please—that the object over there is red. But over and above this there is, of course, the aspect which many philosophers have attempted to clarify by the notion of *impressions* or *immediate experience.*

It was pointed out in Sections 21 ff. above that there are prima facie two ways in which facts of the form *x merely looks red* might be explained, in addition to the kind of explanation which is based on empirical generalizations relating the color of objects, the circumstances in which they are seen, and the colors they look to have. These two ways are (a) the introduction of impressions or immediate experiences as theoretical entities; and (b) the *discovery*, on scrutinizing these situations, that they contain impressions or immediate experiences as components. I called attention to the paradoxical character of the first of these alternatives, and refused, at that time, to take it seriously. But in the meantime the second alternative, involving as it does the Myth of the Given, has turned out to be no more satisfactory.

For, in the first place, how are these impressions to be described, if not by using such words as "red" and "triangular." Yet, if my argument, to date, is sound, physical objects alone can be literally red and triangular. Thus, in the cases I am considering, there is nothing to be red and triangular. It would seem to follow that "impression of a red triangle" could mean nothing more than "impression of *the sort which* is common to those experiences in which we either see that something is red and triangular, or something merely looks red and triangular or there merely looks to be a red and triangular object over there." And if we can never characterize "impressions" intrinsically, but only by what is logically a definite description, i.e., *as the kind of entity which* is common to such situations, then we would scarcely seem to be any better off than if we maintained that talk about "impressions" is a notational convenience, a code, for the language in which we speak of how things look and what there looks to be.

And this line of thought is reinforced by the consideration

that once we give up the idea that we begin our sojourn in this world with any—even a vague, fragmentary, and undiscriminating—awareness of the logical space of particulars, kinds, facts, and resemblances, and recognize that even such "simple" concepts as those of colors are the fruit of a long process of publicly reinforced responses to public objects (including verbal performances) in public situations, we may well be puzzled as to how, even if there are such things as impressions or sensations, we could come to know that there are, and to know what sort of thing they are. *For we now recognize that instead of coming to have a concept of something because we have noticed that sort of thing, to have the ability to notice a sort of thing is already to have the concept of that sort of thing, and cannot account for it.*

Indeed, once we think this line of reasoning through, we are struck by the fact that if it is sound, we are faced not only with the question "How could we come to have the idea of an 'impression' or 'sensation?'" but by the question "How could we come to have the idea of something's looking red to us, or," to get to the crux of the matter, "of seeing that something is red?" In short, we are brought face to face with the general problem of understanding how there can be *inner episodes*—episodes, that is, which somehow combine *privacy*, in that each of us has privileged access to his own, with *intersubjectivity*, in that each of us can, in principle, know about the other's. We might try to put this more linguistically as the problem of how there can be a sentence (e.g. "S has a toothache") of which it is *logically* true that whereas *anybody* can use it to state a fact, only *one* person, namely S himself, can use it to make a report. But while this is a useful formulation, it does not do justice to the supposedly *episodic* character of the items in question. And that this is the heart of the puzzle is shown by the fact that many philosophers who would not deny that there are short-term hypothetical and mongrel hypothetical-categorical facts about behavior which others can ascribe to us on behavioral evidence, but which only *we* can *report*, have found it to be logical nonsense to speak of non-behavioral *episodes* of which this is true. Thus, it has been claimed by Ryle (17) that the very idea that there are such episodes is a category mistake, while others have argued that though there are such episodes, they cannot be characterized in intersubjective discourse, learned as it is in a context of public objects and in the 'academy' of one's linguistic peers. It is my purpose to argue that both these contentions are quite mistaken, and that not only are inner episodes *not* category mistakes, they are quite "effable" in intersubjective discourse. And it is my purpose to show, positively, *how* this can be the case. I am particularly concerned to make this point in connection with such inner episodes as sensations and feelings, in short, with what has — unfortunately, I think — been called "immediate experience." For such an account is necessary to round off this examination of the Myth of the Given. But before I can come to grips with these topics, the way must be prepared by a discussion of inner episodes of quite another kind, namely *thoughts.* .

## XI. Thoughts: The Classical View

**46.** Recent empiricism has been of two minds about the status of *thoughts*. On the one hand, it has resonated to the idea that insofar as there are *episodes* which are thoughts, they are *verbal* or *linguistic* episodes. Clearly, however, even if candid overt verbal behaviors by people who had learned a language *were* thoughts, there are not nearly enough of them to account for all the cases in which it would be argued that a person was thinking. Nor can we plausibly suppose that the remainder is accounted for by those inner episodes which are often very clumsily lumped together under the heading "verbal imagery."

On the other hand, they have been tempted to suppose that the *episodes* which are referred to by verbs pertaining to thinking include all forms of "intelligent behavior," verbal as well as nonverbal, and that the "thought episodes" which are supposed to be manifested by these behaviors are not really episodes at all, but rather hypothetical and mongrel hypothetical-categorical facts about these and still other behaviors. This, however, runs into the difficulty that whenever we try to explain what we mean by calling a piece of *nonhabitual* behavior intelligent, we seem to find it necessary to do so in terms of *thinking*. The uncomfortable feeling will not be downed that the dispositional account of thoughts in terms of intelligent behavior is covertly circular.

**47.** Now the classical tradition claimed that there is a family of episodes, neither overt verbal behavior nor verbal imagery, which are *thoughts*, and that both overt verbal behavior and verbal imagery owe their meaningfulness to the fact that they stand to these *thoughts* in the unique relation of "expressing" them. These episodes are introspectable. Indeed, it was usually believed that they could not occur without being known to occur. But this can be traced to a number of confusions, perhaps the most important of which was the idea that *thoughts* belong in the same general category as sensations, images, tickles, itches, etc. This mis-assimilation of thoughts to sensations and feelings was equally, as we saw in Sections 26 ff. above, a mis-assimilation of sensations and feelings to thoughts, and a falsification of both. The assump-

tion that if there are thought episodes, they must be immediate experiences is common both to those who propounded
the classical view and to those who reject it, saying that they
"find no such experiences." If we purge the classical tradition of these confusions, it becomes the idea that to each of
us belongs a stream of episodes, not themselves immediate experiences, to which we have privileged, but by no
means either invariable or infallible, access. These episodes
can occur without being "expressed" by overt verbal behavior, though verbal behavior is—in an important sense—their
natural fruition. Again, we can "hear ourselves think," but
the verbal imagery which enables us to do this is no more
the thinking itself than is the overt verbal behavior by which
it is expressed and communicated to others. It is a mistake
to suppose that we must be having verbal imagery—indeed,
any imagery—when we "know what we are thinking"—in
short, to suppose that "privileged access" must be construed
on a perceptual or quasi-perceptual model.

Now, it is my purpose to defend such a revised classical
analysis of our common-sense conception of thoughts, and
in the course of doing so I shall develop distinctions which
will later contribute to a resolution, in principle, of the puzzle
of *immediate experience.* But before I continue, let me hasten
to add that it will turn out that the view I am about to
expound could, with equal appropriateness, be represented
as a modified form of the view that thoughts are *linguistic*
episodes.

## XII. Our Rylean Ancestors

**48.** But, the reader may well ask, in what sense can these
episodes be "inner" if they are not immediate experiences?

and in what sense can they be "linguistic" if they are neither overt linguistic performances, nor verbal imagery *"in foro interno"*? I am going to answer these and the other questions I have been raising by making a myth of my own, or, to give it an air of up-to-date respectability, by writing a piece of science fiction—anthropological science fiction. Imagine a stage in pre-history in which humans are limited to what I shall call a Rylean language, a language of which the fundamental descriptive vocabulary speaks of public properties of public objects located in Space and enduring through Time. Let me hasten to add that it is also Rylean in that although its basic resources are limited (how limited I shall be discussing in a moment), its total expressive power is very great. For it makes subtle use not only of the elementary logical operations of conjunction, disjunction, negation, and quantification, but especially of the subjunctive conditional. Furthermore, I shall suppose it to be characterized by the presence of the looser logical relations typical of ordinary discourse which are referred to by philosophers under the headings "vagueness" and "open texture."

I am beginning my myth *in medias res* with humans who have already mastered a Rylean language, because the philosophical situation it is designed to clarify is one in which we are not puzzled by how people acquire a language for referring to public properties of public objects, but are very puzzled indeed about how we learn to speak of inner episodes and immediate experiences.

There are, I suppose, still some philosophers who are inclined to think that by allowing these mythical ancestors of ours the use *ad libitum* of subjunctive conditionals, we have, in effect, enabled them to say anything that *we* can say when we speak of *thoughts, experiences* (seeing, hearing, etc.), and *immediate experiences*. I doubt that there are many. In any case, the story I am telling is designed to show exactly *how* the idea that an intersubjective language *must* be Rylean rests on too simple a picture of the relation of intersubjective discourse to public objects.

**49.** The questions I am, in effect, raising are "What resources would have to be added to the Rylean language of these talking animals in order that they might come to recognize each other and themselves as animals that *think, observe*, and have *feelings* and *sensations*, as we use these terms?" and "How could the addition of these resources be construed as reasonable?" In the first place, the language would have to be enriched with the fundamental resources of semantical discourse—that is to say, the resources necessary for making such characteristically semantical statements as "*'Rot'* means red," and "*'Der Mond ist rund'* is true if and only if the moon is round." It is sometimes said, e.g., by Carnap (6), that these resources can be constructed out of the vocabulary of formal logic, and that they would therefore already be contained, in principle, in our Rylean language. I have criticized this idea in another place (20) and shall not discuss it here. In any event, a decision on this point is not essential to the argument.

Let it be granted, then, that these mythical ancestors of ours are able to characterize each other's verbal behavior in semantical terms; that, in other words, they not only can talk about each other's predictions as causes and effects, and as indicators (with greater or less reliability) of other verbal and nonverbal states of affairs, but can also say of these verbal productions that they *mean* thus and so, that they say *that* such and such, that they are true, false, etc. And let me emphasize, as was pointed out in Section 31 above, that to make a semantical statement about a verbal event is not a shorthand way of talking about its causes and effects, although there is a sense of "imply" in which semantical statements about verbal productions do *imply* information about the causes and effects of these productions. Thus, when I say "*'Es regnet'* means it is raining," my statement "implies" that the causes and effects of utterances of *"Es regnet"* beyond the Rhine parallel the causes and effects of utterances of "It is raining" by myself and other members of the English-speaking community. And if it didn't imply this, it couldn't perform its role. But this is not to say that semantical statements are definitional shorthand for statements about the causes and effects of verbal performances.

**50.** With the resources of semantical discourse, the language of our fictional ancestors has acquired a dimension which gives considerably more plausibility to the claim that they are in a position to talk about *thoughts* just as we are. For characteristic of thoughts is their *intentionality, reference,* or *aboutness,* and it is clear that semantical talk about the meaning or reference of verbal expressions has the same structure as mentalistic discourse concerning what thoughts are about. It is therefore all the more tempting to suppose that the intentionality of *thoughts* can be traced to the application of semantical categories to overt verbal performances, and to suggest a modified Rylean account according to which talk about so-called "thoughts" is shorthand for hypothetical and mongrel categorical-hypothetical statements about overt verbal and nonverbal behavior, *and* that talk about the *intentionality* of these "episodes" is correspondingly reducible to semantical talk about the verbal components.

What is the alternative? Classically it has been the idea that not only are there overt verbal episodes which can be characterized in semantical terms, but, *over and above these,* there are certain inner episodes which are properly characterized by the traditional vocabulary of *intentionality.* And, of course, the classical scheme includes the idea that semantical discourse about overt verbal performances is to be analyzed in terms of talk about the intentionality of the mental episodes which are "expressed" by these overt performances. My immediate problem is to see if I can reconcile the classical idea of thoughts as inner episodes which are neither overt behavior nor verbal imagery and which are properly referred to in terms of the vocabulary of intentionality, with the idea that the categories of intentionality are, at bottom, semantical categories pertaining to overt verbal performances.*

## XIII. Theories and Models

**51.** But what might these episodes be? And, in terms of our science fiction, how might our ancestors have come to recognize their existence? The answer to these questions is surprisingly straightforward, once the logical space of our discussion is enlarged to include a distinction, central to the philosophy of science, between the language of *theory* and the language of *observation.* Although this distinction is a familiar one, I shall take a few paragraphs to highlight those aspects of the distinction which are of greatest relevance to our problem.

Informally, to construct a theory is, in its most developed or sophisticated form, to postulate a domain of entities which behave in certain ways set down by the fundamental

---

* An earlier attempt along these lines is to be found in (18) and (19).

principles of the theory, and to correlate—perhaps, in a certain sense to identify—complexes of these theoretical entities with certain non-theoretical objects or situations; that is to say, with objects or situations which are either matters of observable fact or, in principle at least, describable in observational terms. This "correlation" or "identification" of theoretical with observational states of affairs is a tentative one "until further notice," and amounts, so to speak, to erecting temporary bridges which permit the passage from sentences in observational discourse to sentences in the theory, and vice versa. Thus, for example, in the kinetic theory of gases, empirical statements of the form "Gas g at such and such a place and time has such and such a volume, pressure, and temperature" are correlated with theoretical statements specifying certain statistical measures of populations of molecules. These temporary bridges are so set up that inductively established laws pertaining to gases, formulated in the language of observable fact, are correlated with derived propositions or theorems in the language of the theory, and that no proposition in the theory is correlated with a falsified empirical generalization. Thus, a good theory (at least of the type we are considering) "explains" established empirical laws by deriving theoretical counterparts of these laws from a small set of postulates relating to unobserved entities.

These remarks, of course, barely scratch the surface of the problem of the status of theories in scientific discourse. And no sooner have I made them, than I must hasten to qualify them—almost beyond recognition. For while this by now classical account of the nature of theories (one of the earlier formulations of which is due to Norman Campbell (5), and which is to be found more recently in the writings of Carnap

(8), Reichenbach (15, 16), Hempel (10), and Braithwaite (3)) does throw light on the logical status of theories, it emphasizes certain features at the expense of others. By speaking of the construction of a theory as the elaboration of a postulate system which is tentatively correlated with observational discourse, it gives a highly artificial and unrealistic picture of what scientists have actually done in the process of constructing theories. I don't wish to deny that logically sophisticated scientists today *might* and perhaps, on occasion, *do* proceed in true logistical style. I do, however, wish to emphasize two points:

(1) The first is that the fundamental assumptions of a theory are usually developed not by constructing uninterpreted calculi which might correlate in the desired manner with observational discourse, but rather by attempting to find a *model,* i.e. to describe a domain of familiar objects behaving in familiar ways such that we can see how the phenomena to be explained would arise if they consisted of this sort of thing. The essential thing about a model is that it is accompanied, so to speak, by a commentary which *qualifies* or *limits* — but not precisely nor in all respects — the analogy between the familiar objects and the entities which are being introduced by the theory. It is the descriptions of the fundamental ways in which the objects in the model domain, thus qualified, behave, which, transferred to the theoretical entities, correspond to the postulates of the logistical picture of theory construction.

(2) But even more important for our purposes is the fact that the logistical picture of theory construction obscures the most important thing of all, namely that the process of devising "theoretical" explanations of observable phenomena did not spring full-blown from the head of modern science.

In particular, it obscures the fact that not all common-sense inductive inferences are of the form

> All observed A's have been B, *therefore (probably)* all A's are B.

or its statistical counterparts, and leads one mistakenly to suppose that so-called "hypothetic-deductive" explanation is limited to the sophisticated stages of science. The truth of the matter, as I shall shortly be illustrating, is that science is continuous with common sense, and the ways in which the scientist seeks to explain empirical phenomena are refinements of the ways in which plain men, however crudely and schematically, have attempted to understand their environment and their fellow men since the dawn of intelligence. It is this point which I wish to stress at the present time, for I am going to argue that the distinction between theoretical and observational discourse is involved in the logic of concepts pertaining to inner episodes. I say "involved in" for it would be paradoxical and, indeed, incorrect, to say that these concepts *are* theoretical concepts.

52. Now I think it fair to say that some light has already been thrown on the expression "inner episodes"; for while it would indeed be a category mistake to suppose that the inflammability of a piece of wood is, so to speak, a hidden burning which becomes overt or manifest when the wood is placed on the fire, not all the unobservable episodes we suppose to go on in the world are the offspring of category mistakes. Clearly it is by no means an illegitimate use of "in"—though it is a use which has its own logical grammar—to say, for example, that "in" the air around us there are innumerable molecules which, in spite of the observable stodginess of the air, are participating in a veritable turmoil

of episodes. Clearly, the sense in which these episodes are "in" the air is to be explicated in terms of the sense in which the air "is" a population of molecules, and this, in turn, in terms of the logic of the relation between theoretical and observational discourse.

I shall have more to say on this topic in a moment. In the meantime, let us return to our mythical ancestors. It will not surprise my readers to learn that the second stage in the enrichment of their Rylean language is the addition of theoretical discourse. Thus we may suppose these language-using animals to elaborate, without methodological sophistication, crude, sketchy, and vague theories to explain why things which are similar in their observable properties differ in their causal properties, and things which are similar in their causal properties differ in their observable properties.

## XIV. Methodological versus Philosophical Behaviorism

**53.** But we are approaching the time for the central episode in our myth. I want you to suppose that in this Neo-Rylean culture there now appears a genius—let us call him Jones—who is an unsung fore-runner of the movement in psychology, once revolutionary, now commonplace, known as Behaviorism. Let me emphasize that what I have in mind is Behaviorism as a methodological thesis, which I shall be concerned to formulate. For the central and guiding theme in the historical complex known by this term has been a certain conception, or family of conceptions, of how to go about building a science of psychology.

Philosophers have sometimes supposed that Behaviorists are, as such, committed to the idea that our ordinary mentalistic concepts are *analyzable* in terms of overt behavior. But although behaviorism has often been characterized by a certain metaphysical bias, it is not a thesis about the *analysis* of *existing* psychological concepts, but one which concerns the construction of new concepts. As a methodological thesis, it involves no commitment whatever concerning the logical analysis of common-sense mentalistic discourse, nor does it involve a denial that each of us has a privileged access to our state of mind, nor that these states of mind can properly be described in terms of such common-sense concepts as believing, wondering, doubting, intending, wishing, inferring, etc. If we permit ourselves to speak of this privileged access to our states of mind as "introspection," avoiding the implication that there is a "means" whereby we "see" what is going on "inside," as we see external circumstances by the eye, then we can say that Behaviorism, as I shall use the term, does not deny that there is such a thing as introspection, nor that it is, on some topics, at least, quite reliable. The essential point about 'introspection' from the standpoint of Behaviorism is that *we introspect in terms of common sense mentalistic concepts*. And while the Behaviorist admits, as anyone must, that much knowledge is embodied in common-sense mentalistic discourse, and that still more can be gained in the future by formulating and testing hypotheses in terms of them, and while he admits that it is perfectly legitimate to call such a psychology "scientific," he proposes, for his own part, to make no more than a heuristic use of mentalistic discourse, and to construct his concepts "from scratch" in the course of developing his own scientific account of the observable behavior of human organisms.

**54.** But while it is quite clear that scientific Behaviorism is *not* the thesis that common-sense psychological concepts are *analyzable* into concepts pertaining to overt behavior—a thesis which has been maintained by some philosophers and which may be called 'analytical' or 'philosophical' Behaviorism — it is often thought that Behaviorism is committed to the idea that the concepts of a behavioristic psychology must be so analyzable, or, to put things right side up, that properly introduced behavioristic concepts must be built by explicit definition — in the broadest sense — from a basic vocabulary pertaining to overt behavior. The Behaviorist would thus be saying "Whether or not the mentalistic concepts of everyday life are definable in terms of overt behavior, I shall ensure that this is true of the concepts that I shall employ." And it must be confessed that many behavioristically oriented psychologists have believed themselves committed to this austere program of concept formation.

Now I think it reasonable to say that, *thus conceived*, the behavioristic program would be unduly restrictive. Certainly, nothing in the nature of sound scientific procedure requires this self-denial. Physics, the methodological sophistication of which has so impressed — indeed, overly impressed — the other sciences, does not lay down a corresponding restriction on its concepts, nor has chemistry been built in terms of concepts explicitly definable in terms of the observable properties and behavior of chemical substances. The point I am making should now be clear. The behavioristic requirement that all concepts should be *introduced* in terms of a basic vocabulary pertaining to overt behavior is compatible with the idea that some behavioristic concepts are to be introduced as *theoretical* concepts.

**55.** It is essential to note that the theoretical terms of a behavioristic psychology are not only *not* defined in terms of overt behavior, they are also *not* defined in terms of nerves, synapses, neural impulses, etc., etc. A behavioristic theory of

behavior is not, as such, a physiological explanation of behavior. The ability of a framework of theoretical concepts
and propositions successfully to explain behavioral phenomena is logically independent of the identification of these
theoretical concepts with concepts of neurophysiology. What
*is* true—and this is a logical point—is that each special
science dealing with some aspect of the human organism
operates within the frame of a certain regulative ideal, the
ideal of a coherent system in which the achievements of each
have an intelligible place. Thus, it is part of the Behaviorist's
business to keep an eye on the total picture of the human
organism which is beginning to emerge. And if the tendency
to premature identification is held in check, there may be
considerable heuristic value in speculative attempts at integration; though, until recently, at least, neurophysiological
speculations in behavior theory have not been particularly
fruitful. And while it is, I suppose, noncontroversial that
when the total scientific picture of man and his behavior is
in, it will involve *some* identification of concepts in behavior
theory with concepts pertaining to the functioning of ana-
tomical structures, it should not be assumed that behavior
theory is committed *ab initio* to a physiological identification
of *all* its concepts,—that its concepts are, so to speak, physiological from the start.

We have, in effect, been distinguishing between two dimensions of the logic (or 'methodologic') of theoretical terms:
(a) their role in explaining the selected phenomena of which
the theory is the theory; (b) their role as candidates for
integration in what we have called the "total picture." These
roles are equally part of the logic, and hence the "meaning,"
of theoretical terms. Thus, at any one time the terms in a
theory will carry with them as part of their logical force that

which it is reasonable to envisage—whether schematically or determinately—as the manner of their integration. However, for the purposes of my argument, it will be useful to refer to these two roles as though it were a matter of a distinction between what I shall call *pure theoretical concepts*, and hypotheses concerning the relation of these concepts to concepts in other specialties. What we *can* say is that the less a scientist is in a position to conjecture about the way in which a certain theory can be expected to integrate with other specialities, the more the concepts of his theory approximate to the status of pure theoretical concepts. To illustrate: We can imagine that Chemistry developed a sophisticated and successful theory to explain chemical phenomena before either electrical or magnetic phenomena were noticed; and that chemists developed as pure theoretical concepts, certain concepts which it later became reasonable to identify with concepts belonging to the framework of electromagnetic theory.

## XV. The Logic of Private Episodes: Thoughts

**56.** With these all too sketchy remarks on Methodological Behaviorism under our belts, let us return once again to our fictional ancestors. We are now in a position to characterize the original Rylean language in which they described themselves and their fellows as not only a *behavioristic* language, but a behavioristic language which is restricted to the *non-theoretical* vocabulary of a behavioristic psychology. Suppose, now, that in the attempt to account for the fact that his fellow men behave intelligently not only when their conduct is threaded on a string of overt verbal episodes—that is to say, as *we* would put it, when they "think out loud"—but also when no detectable verbal output is present, Jones develops a *theory* according to which overt utterances are but the culmination of a process which begins with certain inner episodes. *And let us suppose that his model for these episodes* which initiate the events which culminate in overt verbal behavior *is that of overt verbal behavior itself. In other words, using the language of the model, the theory is to the effect that overt verbal behavior is the culmination of a process which begins with "inner speech."*

It is essential to bear in mind that what Jones means by "inner speech" is not to be confused with *verbal imagery*. As a matter of fact, Jones, like his fellows, does not as yet even have the concept of an image.

It is easy to see the general lines a Jonesean theory will take. According to it the true cause of intelligent nonhabitual behavior is "inner speech." Thus, even when a hungry person overtly says "Here is an edible object" and proceeds to eat it, the true—theoretical—cause of his eating, given his hunger, is not the overt utterance, but the "inner utterance of this sentence."

**57.** The first thing to note about the Jonesean theory is that, as built on the model of speech episodes, *it carries over to these inner episodes the applicability of semantical categories.* Thus, just as Jones has, like his fellows, been speaking of overt utterances as *meaning* this or that, or being *about* this or that, so he now speaks of these inner episodes as *meaning* this or that, or being *about* this or that.

The second point to remember is that although Jones' theory involves a *model,* it is not identical with it. Like all theories formulated in terms of a model, it also includes a *commentary* on the model; a commentary which places more or less sharply drawn restrictions on the analogy between the theoretical entities and the entities of the model. Thus,

while his theory talks of "inner speech," the commentary
hastens to add that, of course, the episodes in question are
not the wagging of a hidden tongue, nor are any sounds
produced by this "inner speech."

**58.** The general drift of my story should now be clear. I
shall therefore proceed to make the essential points quite
briefly:

(1) What we must suppose Jones to have developed is the
germ of a theory which permits many different develop-
ments. We must not pin it down to any of the more sophisticated forms it takes in the hands of classical philosophers.
Thus, the theory need not be given a Socratic or Cartesian
form, according to which this "inner speech" is a function of
a separate substance; though primitive peoples may have had
good reason to suppose that humans consist of two separate
things.

(2) Let us suppose Jones to have called these discursive
entities *thoughts*. We can admit at once that the framework
of thoughts he has introduced is a framework of "unobserved," "nonempirical" "inner" episodes. For we can point
out immediately that in these respects they are no worse off
than the particles and episodes of physical theory. For these
episodes are "in" language-using animals as molecular im-
pacts are "in" gases, not as "ghosts" are in "machines." They
are "nonempirical" in the simple sense that they are *theoretical*—not definable in observational terms. Nor does the fact
that they are, *as introduced*, unobserved entities imply that
Jones could not have good reason for supposing them to
exist. Their "purity" is not a *metaphysical* purity, but, so to
speak, a *methodological* purity. As we have seen, the fact that
they are not introduced as physiological entities does not
preclude the possibility that at a later methodological stage,

they may, so to speak, "turn out" to be such. Thus, there are
many who would say that it is already reasonable to suppose
that these *thoughts* are to be "identified" with complex events
in the cerebral cortex functioning along the lines of a calcu-
lating machine. Jones, of course, has no such idea.

(3) Although the theory postulates that overt discourse is
the culmination of a process which begins with "inner discourse," this should not be taken to mean that overt discourse
stands to "inner discourse" *as voluntary movements stand to
intentions and motives.* True, overt linguistic events *can* be
produced as means to ends. But serious errors creep into the
interpretation of both language and thought if one interprets
the idea that overt linguistic episodes *express* thoughts, on the
model of the use of an instrument. Thus, it should be noted
that Jones' theory, as I have sketched it, is perfectly compatible with the idea that the ability to have thoughts is
acquired in the process of acquiring overt speech and that
only after overt speech is well established, can "inner speech"
occur without its overt culmination.

(4) Although the occurrence of overt speech episodes
which are characterizable in semantical terms is explained
by the theory in terms of *thoughts* which are *also* characterized
in semantical terms, this does not mean that the idea that
overt speech "has meaning" is being *analyzed* in terms of the
intentionality of thoughts. It must not be forgotten that *the
semantical characterization of overt verbal episodes is the primary use
of semantical terms, and that overt linguistic events as semantically
characterized are the model for the inner episodes introduced by the
theory.*

(5) One final point before we come to the dénouement of
the first episode in the saga of Jones. It cannot be emphasized too much that although these theoretical discursive

episodes or *thoughts* are introduced as *inner* episodes—which is merely to repeat that they are introduced as *theoretical* episodes—they are *not* introduced as *immediate experiences*. Let me remind the reader that Jones, like his Neo-Rylean contemporaries, does not as yet have this concept. And even when he, and they, acquire it, by a process which will be the second episode in my myth, it will only be the philosophers among them who will suppose that the inner episodes introduced for one theoretical purpose—thoughts—must be a subset of immediate experiences, inner episodes introduced for another theoretical purpose.

59. Here, then, is the *dénouement*. I have suggested a number of times that although it would be most misleading to say that concepts pertaining to thinking are theoretical concepts, yet their status might be illuminated by means of the contrast between theoretical and non-theoretical discourse. We are now in a position to see exactly why this is so. For once our fictitious ancestor, Jones, has developed the theory that overt verbal behavior is the expression of thoughts, and taught his compatriots to make use of the theory in interpreting each other's behavior, it is but a short step to the use of this language in self-description. Thus, when Tom, watching Dick, has behavioral evidence which warrants the use of the sentence (in the language of the theory) "Dick is thinking 'p'" (or "Dick is thinking that p"), Dick, using the same behavioral evidence, can say, in the language of the theory, "I am thinking 'p'" (or "I am thinking that p"). And it now turns out—need it have?—that Dick can be trained to give reasonably reliable self-descriptions, using the language of the theory, without having to observe his overt behavior. Jones brings this about, roughly, by applauding utterances by Dick of "I am thinking that p" when the behavioral evidence strongly supports the theoretical statement "Dick is

thinking that p"; and by frowning on utterances of "I am thinking that p," when the evidence does not support this theoretical statement. Our ancestors begin to speak of the privileged access each of us has to his own thoughts. *What began as a language with a purely theoretical use has gained a reporting role.*

As I see it, this story helps us understand that concepts pertaining to such inner episodes as thoughts are primarily and essentially *intersubjective*, as intersubjective as the concept of a positron, and that the reporting role of these concepts—the fact that each of us has a privileged access to his thoughts—constitutes a dimension of the use of these concepts which is *built on* and *presupposes* this intersubjective status. My myth has shown that the fact that language is essentially an *intersubjective* achievement, and is learned in intersubjective contexts—a fact rightly stressed in modern psychologies of language, thus by B. F. Skinner (21), and by certain philosophers, e.g. Carnap (7), Wittgenstein (22)—is compatible with the "privacy" of "inner episodes." It also makes clear that this privacy is not an "absolute privacy." For if it recognizes that these concepts have a reporting use in which one is not drawing inferences from behavioral evidence, it nevertheless insists that the fact that overt behavior *is* evidence for these episodes *is built into the very logic of these concepts,* just as the fact that the observable behavior of gases is evidence for molecular episodes is built into the very logic of molecule talk.

## XVI. The Logic of Private Episodes: Impressions

**60.** We are now ready for the problem of the status of concepts pertaining to immediate experience. The first step is to remind ourselves that among the inner episodes which belong to the framework of *thoughts* will be perceptions, that is to say, *seeing that the table is brown, hearing that the piano is out of tune*, etc. Until Jones introduced this framework, the only concepts our fictitious ancestors had of perceptual *episodes* were those of overt verbal *reports*, made, for example, in the context of looking at an object in standard conditions. *Seeing that something is the case* is an inner episode in the Jonesean theory which has as its model *reporting on looking that something is the case*. It will be remembered from an earlier section that just as when I say that Dick *reported* that the table is green, I commit myself to the truth of what he reported, so to say of Dick that he *saw* that the table is green is, in part, to ascribe to Dick the idea '*this* table is green' and to endorse this idea. The reader might refer back to Sections 16 ff. for an elaboration of this point.

With the enrichment of the originally Rylean framework to include inner perceptual episodes, I have established contact with my original formulation of the problem of inner experience (Sections 22 ff.). For I can readily reconstruct in this framework my earlier account of the *language of appearing*, both *qualitative* and *existential*. Let us turn, therefore to the final chapter of our historical novel. By now our ancestors speak a quite un-Rylean language. But it still contains no reference to such things as impressions, sensations, or feelings—in short, to the items which philosophers lump together under the heading "immediate experiences." It will be remembered that we had reached a point at which, as far as we could see, the phrase "impression of a red triangle" could only mean something like "that state of a perceiver—over and above the idea that there is a red and triangular physical object over there—which is common to those situations in which

(a) he sees that the object over there is red and triangular;

(b) the object over there looks to him to be red and triangular;

(c) there looks to him to be a red and triangular physical object over there."

Our problem was that, on the one hand, it seemed absurd to say that impressions, for example, are theoretical entities, while, on the other, the interpretation of impressions as theoretical entities seemed to provide the only hope of accounting for the positive content and explanatory power that the idea that there are such entities appears to have, and of enabling us to understand how we could have arrived at this idea. The account I have just been giving of *thoughts* suggests how this apparent dilemma can be resolved.

For we continue the myth by supposing that Jones develops, in crude and sketchy form, of course, a theory of sense perception. Jones' theory does not have to be either well-articulated or precise in order to be the first effective step in the development of a mode of discourse which today, in the case of some sense-modalities at least, is extraordinarily subtle and complex. We need, therefore, attribute to this mythical theory only those minimal features which enable it to throw light on the logic of our ordinary language about immediate experiences. From this standpoint it is sufficient to suppose that the hero of my myth postulates a class of inner—theoretical—episodes which he calls, say, *impressions*, and which are the end results of the impingement of physical objects and processes on various parts of the body, and, in particular, to follow up the specific form in which I have posed our problem, the eye.

**61.** A number of points can be made right away:

(1) The entities introduced by the theory are *states* of the perceiving subject, *not a class of particulars*. It cannot be emphasized too strongly that the particulars of the common-sense world are such things as books, pages, turnips, dogs, persons, noises, flashes, etc., and the Space and Time—Kant's *Undinge*—in which they come to be. What is likely to make us suppose that *impressions* are introduced as particulars is that, as in the case of thoughts, this ur-theory is formulated in terms of a *model*. This time the model is the idea of a domain of "inner replicas" which, when brought about in standard conditions, share the perceptible characteristics of their physical source. It is important to see that the model is the occurrence "in" perceivers of *replicas*, not of *perceivings of replicas*. Thus, the model for an impression of a red triangle is a *red and triangular replica*, not a *seeing of a red and triangular replica*. The latter alternative would have the merit of recognizing that impressions are not particulars. But, by misunderstanding the role of models in the formulation of a theory, it mistakenly assumes that if the entities of the model are particulars, the theoretical entities which are introduced by means of the model must themselves be particulars—thus overlooking the role of the commentary. And by taking the model to be *seeing a red and triangular replica*, it smuggles into the language of impressions the logic of the language of thoughts. For seeing is a *cognitive* episode which involves the framework of thoughts, and to take it as the model is to give aid and comfort to the assimilation of impressions to thoughts, and thoughts to impressions which, as I have already pointed out, is responsible for many of the confusions of the classical account of both thoughts and impressions.

(2) The fact that *impressions* are theoretical entities en-

ables us to understand how they can be *intrinsically* characterized—that is to say, characterized by something more than
a *definite description*, such as "entity of *the kind which* has as its
standard cause looking at a red and triangular physical object
in such and such circumstances" or "entity of *the kind which*
is common to the situations in which there looks to be a red
and triangular physical object." For although the predicates
of a theory owe their meaningfulness to the fact that they are
logically related to predicates which apply to the observable
phenomena which the theory explains, the predicates of a
theory are not shorthand for definite descriptions of properties in terms of these observation predicates. When the kinetic theory of gases speaks of molecules as having *mass*, the
term "mass" is not the abbreviation of a definite description
of the form "the property which . . ." Thus, "impression of a
red triangle" does not simply mean "impression such as is
caused by red and triangular physical objects in standard
conditions," though it is true—*logically* true—of impressions
of red triangles that they are of that sort which *is* caused by
red and triangular objects in standard conditions.

(3) If the theory of impressions were developed in true
logistical style, we could say that the intrinsic properties of
impressions are "implicitly defined" by the postulates of the
theory, as we can say that the intrinsic properties of subatomic particles are "implicitly defined" by the fundamental
principles of subatomic theory. For this would be just another way of saying that one knows the meaning of a theoretical term when one knows (a) how it is related to other
theoretical terms, and (b) how the theoretical system as a
whole is tied to the observation language. But, as I have
pointed out, our ur-behaviorist does not formulate his theory
in textbook style. He formulates it in terms of a model.

Now the model entities are entities which *do* have intrinsic properties. They are, for example, red and triangular wafers. It might therefore seem that the theory specifies the intrinsic characteristics of impressions to be the familiar perceptible qualities of physical objects and processes. If this were so, of course, the theory would be ultimately incoherent, for it would attribute to impressions—which are clearly not physical objects—characteristics which, if our argument to date is sound, only physical objects can have. Fortunately, this line of thought overlooks what we have called the commentary on the model, which qualifies, restricts and interprets the analogy between the familiar entities of the model and the theoretical entities which are being introduced. Thus, it would be a mistake to suppose that since the *model* for the impression of a red triangle is a red and triangular wafer, the impression itself is a red and triangular wafer. What can be said is that the impression of a red triangle is *analogous*, to an extent which is by no means neatly and tidily specified, to a red and triangular wafer. The *essential* feature of the analogy is that visual impressions stand to one another in a system of ways of resembling and differing which is structurally similar to the ways in which the colors and shapes of visible objects resemble and differ.

(4) It might be concluded from this last point that the concept of the impression of a red triangle is a "purely formal" concept, the concept of a "logical form" which can acquire a "content" only by means of "ostensive definition." One can see why a philosopher might want to say this, and why he might conclude that in so far as concepts pertaining to immediate experiences are *intersubjective*, they are "purely structural," the "content" of immediate experience being incommunicable. Yet this line of thought is but another expression of the Myth of the Given. For the theoretical concept

of the impression of a red triangle would be no more and no less "without content" than *any* theoretical concept. And while, like these, it must belong to a framework which is logically connected with the language of observable fact, the logical relation between a theoretical language and the language of observable fact has nothing to do with the epistemological fiction of an "ostensive definition."

(5) The impressions of Jones' theory are, as was pointed out above, states of the perceiver, rather than particulars. If we remind ourselves that these states are not introduced as physiological states (see Section 55), a number of interesting questions arise which tie in with the reflections on the status of the scientific picture of the world (Sections 39–44 above) but which, unfortunately, there is space only to adumbrate. Thus, some philosophers have thought it obvious that we can expect that in the development of science it will become reasonable to identify *all* the concepts of behavior theory with definable terms in neurophysiological theory, and these, in turn, with definable terms in theoretical physics. It is important to realize that the second step of this prediction, at least, is either a *truism* or a *mistake*. It is a truism if it involves a tacit redefinition of "physical theory" to mean "theory adequate to account for the observable behavior of any object (including animals and persons) which has physical properties." While if "physical theory" is taken in its ordinary sense of "theory adequate to explain the observable behavior of physical objects," it is, I believe, mistaken.

To ask how *impressions* fit together with *electromagnetic fields*, for example, is to ask a mistaken question. It is to mix the framework of *molar* behavior theory with the framework of the *micro*-theory of physical objects. The proper question is, rather, "What would correspond in a *micro*-theory of sentient organisms to *molar* concepts pertaining to impressions?" And it is, I believe, in answer to this question that one would come upon the *particulars* which sense-datum theorists profess to find (by analysis) in the common-sense universe of discourse (cf. Section 23). Furthermore, I believe that in characterizing these particulars, the micro-behaviorist would be led to say something like the following: "It is such particulars which (from the standpoint of the theory) are being responded to by the organism when it looks to a *person* as though there were a red and triangular physical object over there." It would, of course, be incorrect to say that, in the ordinary sense, such a particular is red or triangular. What *could* be said,* however, is that whereas in the common-sense picture physical objects are red and triangular but the impression "of" a red triangle is neither red nor triangular, in the framework of this micro-theory, the theoretical counterparts of sentient organisms are Space-Time worms characterized by two kinds of variables: (a) variables which also characterize the theoretical counterparts of *merely* material objects; (b) variables peculiar to sentient things; and that these latter variables are the counterparts in this new framework of the perceptible qualities of the physical objects of the common-sense framework. It is statements such as these which would be the cash value of the idea that "physical objects aren't really colored; colors exist only in the perceiver," and that "to see that the facing surface of a physical object is red and triangular is to *mistake* a red and triangular sense content for a physical object with a red and triangular facing side."

---

* For a discussion of some logical points pertaining to this framework, the reader should consult the essay, "The Concept of Emergence," by Paul E. Meehl and Wilfrid Sellars, *Minnesota Studies in the Philosophy of Science,* vol. 1 (Minneapolis: University of Minnesota Press, 1956), pp. 239–252.

Both these ideas clearly treat what is really a speculative philosophical critique (see Section 41) of the common-sense framework of physical objects and the perception of physical objects in the light of an envisaged ideal scientific framework, as though it were a matter of distinctions which can be drawn *within* the common-sense framework itself.

**62.** This brings me to the final chapter of my story. Let us suppose that as his final service to mankind before he vanishes without a trace, Jones teaches his theory of perception to his fellows. As before in the case of *thoughts*, they begin by using the language of impressions to draw theoretical conclusions from appropriate premises. (Notice that the evidence for theoretical statements in the language of impressions will include such introspectible inner episodes as *its looking to one as though there were a red and triangular physical object over there*, as well as overt behavior.) Finally he succeeds in training them to make a *reporting* use of this language. He trains them, that is, to say "I have the impression of a red triangle" when, and only when, according to the theory, they are indeed having the impression of a red triangle.

Once again the myth helps us to understand that concepts pertaining to certain inner episodes—in this case *impressions*—can be primarily and essentially *intersubjective*, without being resolvable into overt behavioral symptoms, and that the reporting role of these concepts, their role in introspection, the fact that each of us has a privileged access to his impressions, constitutes a dimension of these concepts which is *built on* and *presupposes* their role in intersubjective discourse. It also makes clear why the "privacy" of these episodes is not the "absolute privacy" of the traditional puzzles. For, as in the case of thoughts, the fact that overt behavior is evidence for these episodes is built into the very logic of these concepts as the fact that the observable behavior of gases is evidence for molecular episodes is built into the very logic of molecule talk.

Notice that what our "ancestors" have acquired under the guidance of Jones is not "just another language"—a "notational convenience" or "code"—which merely enables them to say what they can already say in the language of qualitative and existential looking. They have acquired another language, indeed, but it is one which, though it rests on a framework of discourse about public objects in Space and Time, has an autonomous logical structure, and contains an *explanation of,* not just a *code for,* such facts as that *there looks to me to be a red and triangular physical object over there.* And notice that while our "ancestors" came to notice impressions, and the language of impressions embodies a "discovery" that there are such things, the language of impressions was no more tailored to fit *antecedent* noticings of these entities than the language of molecules was tailored to fit antecedent noticings of molecules.

And the spirit of Jones is not yet dead. For it is the particulars of the micro-theory discussed in Section 61 (5) which are the solid core of the sense contents and sense fields of the sense-datum theorist. Envisaging the general lines of that framework, even sketching some of its regions, he has taught himself to play with it (in his study) as a report language. Unfortunately, he mislocates the truth of these conceptions, and, with a modesty forgivable in any but a philosopher, confuses his own creative enrichment of the framework of empirical knowledge, with an analysis of knowledge as it was. He construes as *data* the particulars and arrays of particulars which he has come to be able to observe, and believes them to be antecedent objects of knowledge which have somehow been in the framework from the beginning. It is in the very act of *taking* that he speaks of the *given*.

**63.** I have used a myth to kill a myth—the Myth of the Given. But is my myth really a myth? Or does the reader not recognize Jones as Man himself in the middle of his journey from the grunts and groans of the cave to the subtle and polydimensional discourse of the drawing room, the laboratory, and the study, the language of Henry and William James, of Einstein and of the philosophers who, in their efforts to break out of discourse to an *arché* beyond discourse, have provided the most curious dimension of all.

## References

1. Ayer, A. J. *Foundations of Empirical Knowledge*. London: Macmillan, 1940.
2. Ayer, A. J. "The Terminology of Sense Data," in *Philosophical Essays*, pp. 66–104. London: Macmillan, 1954. Also in *Mind*, 54, 1945, pp. 298–312.
3. Braithwaite, R. B. *Scientific Explanation*. Cambridge: Cambridge Univ. Pr., 1953.
4. Broad, C. D. *Scientific Thought*. London: Kegan Paul, 1923.
5. Campbell, Norman. *Physics: The Elements*. Cambridge: Cambridge Univ. Pr., 1920.
6. Carnap, Rudolf. *Introduction to Semantics*. Chicago: Univ. of Chicago Pr., 1942.
7. Carnap, Rudolf. *"Psychologie in Physikalischer Sprache,"* Erkenntnis, 3:107–42 (1933).
8. Carnap, Rudolf. "The Interpretation of Physics," in H. Feigl and M. Brodbeck (eds.), *Readings in the Philosophy of Science*, pp. 309–18. New York: Appleton-Century-Crofts, 1953. This selection consists of pp. 59–69 of his *Foundations of Logic and Mathematics*. Chicago: Univ. of Chicago Pr., 1939.
9. Chisholm, Roderick. "The Theory of Appearing," in Max Black

(ed.), *Philosophical Analysis*, pp. 102–18. Ithaca: Cornell Univ. Pr., 1950.

10. Hempel, C. G. *Fundamentals of Concept Formation in Empirical Science*. Chicago: Univ. of Chicago Pr., 1952.

11. Linnell, John. "Berkeley's Critique of Abstract Ideas." A Ph.D. thesis submitted to the Graduate Faculty of the University of Minnesota, June 1954.

12. Paul, G. A. "Is there a Problem about Sense Data?" in Supplementary Volume XV of the *Aristotelian Society Proceedings*. Also in A. G. N. Flew (ed.), *Logic and Language*. New York: Philosophical Lib., 1951.

13. Price, H. H. *Perception*. London: Methuen, 1932.

14. Price, H. H. *Thinking and Experience*. London: Hutchinson's Univ. Lib., 1953.

15. Reichenbach, H. *Philosophie der Raum-Zeit-Lehre*. Berlin: de Gruyter, 1928.

16. Reichenbach, H. *Experience and Prediction*. Chicago: Univ. of Chicago Pr., 1938.

17. Ryle, Gilbert. *The Concept of Mind*. London: Hutchinson's Univ. Lib., 1949.

18. Sellars, Wilfrid. "Mind, Meaning and Behavior," *Philosophical Studies*, 3:83–94 (1952).

19. Sellars, Wilfrid. "A Semantical Solution of the Mind-Body Problem," *Methodos*, 5:45–84 (1953).

20. Sellars, Wilfrid. "Empiricism and Abstract Entities," in Paul A. Schlipp (ed.), *The Philosophy of Rudolf Carnap*. Evanston (Ill.): Library of Living Philosophers (forthcoming). (Available in mimeograph form from the author.)

21. Skinner, B. F. "The Operational Analysis of Psychological Terms," *Psychological Review*, 52:270–77 (1945). Reprinted in H. Feigl and M. Brodbeck (eds.), *Readings in the Philosophy of Science*, pp. 585–94. New York: Appleton-Century-Crofts, 1953.

22. Wittgenstein, Ludwig. *Philosophical Investigations*. London: Macmillan, 1953.

# Study Guide

ROBERT BRANDOM

T HE NOTES THAT FOLLOW were developed over the years to help my graduate and advanced undergraduate students at the University of Pittsburgh to see their way through the textual trees to the Sellarsian forest. They are meant to provide only a first take on the material, to indicate the most general outlines of the structure of the essay and of the thought behind it. To that end, many philosophically interesting issues and discussions have been brushed past. In particular, I have sedulously avoided discussing genuinely esoteric issues — such as the philosophical significance some have professed to find in the distinction between 'red' paragraphs and 'green' paragraphs. The formulations and characterizations that are provided are not intended to be definitive or authoritative. They aim to provide a place to start reading this rich and difficult text.

The idea for such a document, and the notes to the concluding sections, had their origins in a handout Richard Rorty circulated for similar purposes when I was a graduate student at Princeton in the 1970s. I am grateful to my colleague John McDowell, and to our former student Danielle Macbeth, for many suggestions and improvements. It should be noted, though, that where their comments evidenced substantive disagreements about what Sellars is (and ought to be) saying—concerning in particular the intricacies of 'looks' talk in relation to reports of the presence of secondary qualities, and the various theses and commitments involved in scientific realism—I have stuck to my own readings. The errors that remain, both those of omission and of commission, should be charged to my account alone.

*Note:* Section numbers of "Empiricism and the Philosophy of Mind" are indicated in square brackets: [36]. On the rare occasions where sections of this guide must be referenced, I use double brackets: [[36]].

## Part I [1]–[7]
## An Ambiguity in Sense-Datum Theories

*Section 1:* Sellars announces that his project is to attack "the whole framework of givenness." By this he does not mean to be undercutting the distinction between judgments we arrive at noninferentially, paradigmatically through perception, and those that are arrived at as the conclusions of inferences. Indeed, one of the positive tasks of the essay is precisely to tell us how to understand noninferential reports without insensibly sliding into the constellation of philosophical commitments that Sellars calls "the Myth of the Given." Sense-datum theories, his immediate target, are important only as prominent and influential instances of the appeal to givenness. We will have to learn to recognize such appeals in many less obvious guises.

In these opening sections, the Myth of the Given shows up in the guise of the idea that some kind of non-epistemic facts about knowers could *entail* epistemic facts about them.[1] Epistemic facts about knowers are in the first instance facts about what someone *knows* (though we will come to see that facts about what one merely *believes* are equally 'epistemic' facts in Sellars's sense). One of Descartes's signal innovations was to define the mind in epistemic terms: for a state to be a *mental* state is for *being* in that state to entail *knowing* that one is in that state (transparency, ruling out ignorance) and for *believing* that one is in that state to entail *being* in that state (incorrigibility, ruling out error). The mind is the realm of what is known *immediately,* not just in the sense of noninferentially, but in the stronger sense that its goings-on are *given* to us in a way that banishes the possibility both of ignorance and of error. (Descartes's thought was that if anything is known to us *mediately,* that is, by means of representations of it, then something — some kind of representations — must be known to us *immediately,* on pain of an infinite regress.) Sellars will try to show us that the Cartesian way of talking about the mind is the result of confusion about the distinction between epistemic and non-epistemic items, and the roles they can play in various sorts of explanation.

In its most familiar form, the Myth of the Given blurs the distinction between sentience and sapience. This is the distinction between being aware in the sense of being merely *awake* (which we share with nondiscursive animals — those

1. The discussion of foundationalism in [32] shows that one can still be committed to the Myth of the Given even if one's foundations are conceived as epistemic facts — if the capacity to know those facts is thought of as independent of inferential capacities and hence the acquisition of ordinary empirical concepts.

that do not grasp concepts), on the one hand, and, on the other hand, being aware in a sense that involves *knowledge* either by *being* a kind of knowledge, or as potentially serving to *justify* judgments that so qualify. The "idea that a sensation of a red triangle is the very paradigm of empirical knowledge" [7] is a paradigm of the sort of conflation in question. The Myth of the Given is the idea that there can be a kind of *awareness* that has two properties. First, it is or entails having a certain sort of *knowledge*—perhaps not of other things, but at least that one is in that state, or a state of that kind—knowledge that the one whose state it is possesses simply in virtue of being in that state. Second, it entails that the capacity to have that sort of awareness, to be in that sort of state, does not presuppose the acquisition of any *concepts*—that one can be aware in that sense independently of and antecedently to grasping or mastering the use of any concepts (paradigmatically through language learning).[2] The conclusion of Sellars's critical argument is that these two features are incompatible: only what is propositionally contentful, and so conceptually articulated, can serve as (or, for that matter, stand in need of) a justification, and so ground or constitute knowledge. Davidson expresses a version of this thought with the slogan, "Nothing can count as a reason for holding a belief except another belief." Sellars's thought is better captured by changing this to "Nothing can count as a reason for endorsing a believable except another believable," where believables are the con-

2. As McDowell puts the point: "The idea of the Given is the idea that the space of reasons, the space of justifications or warrants, extends more widely than the conceptual sphere" (*Mind and World* [Cambridge, Mass.: Harvard University Press, 1994], p. 7); that is, that what is Given can serve as a justification, without its being given requiring the exercise of conceptual capacities.

tents of possible beliefs, that is, what is propositionally contentful.[3]

Sellars understands propositional contentfulness, what is
epistemic in the sense of being a candidate for knowledge,
in terms of role in what he calls "the game of giving and
asking for reasons." "In characterizing an episode or state as
that of *knowing*, we are not giving an empirical description of
that episode or state; we are placing it in the logical space of
reasons, of justifying and being able to justify what one says"
[36]. To treat something as even a candidate for knowledge
is at once to talk about its potential role in *inference*, as
premise and conclusion. Because a crucial distinguishing
feature of epistemic facts for Sellars is that their expression
requires the use of *normative* vocabulary, to treat something
as a candidate for knowledge is also to raise the issue of
its *normative* status. The Myth of the Given eventually appears as "of a piece with the naturalistic fallacy in ethics" —
the attempt to derive *ought* from *is*.[4] This is because talk
of knowledge is inevitably talk of what (conceptually articulated propositional contents) someone is *committed* to,
and whether he is in various senses *entitled* to those commitments.

*Section 2:* Here Sellars distinguishes between the act or episode of sens*ing*, on the one hand, and the content of that

3. The emendation allows that propositionally contentful items that are not
believings might serve as epistemic justifiers — for instance, that *facts* could play this
role.

4. "The idea that epistemic facts can be analyzed without remainder — even 'in
principle' — into non-epistemic facts . . . is . . . a radical mistake — a mistake of a
piece with the so-called 'naturalistic fallacy' in ethics" [5]. This theme arises very
early in Sellars's writing. See, for instance, "A Semantical Solution to the Mind-
Body Problem," reprinted in J. Sicha, ed., *Pure Pragmatics and Possible Worlds: The
Early Essays of Wilfrid Sellars* (Reseda, Calif.: Ridgeview Publishing, 1980).

act, what is sens*ed*, which is called a sense *content,* on the other. When one hallucinates a pink elephant, doing so is sensing, and the sense-content is what makes it an of-a-pink-elephant hallucination, rather than, for instance, an of-a-green-Norway-rat hallucination. In ordinary perception, the contents sensed must be carefully distinguished from the external objects sensed (which are entirely absent in the case of hallucinations).

*Section 3:* Now consider the suitability of sensings of sense contents as foundations of knowledge and justification on the Cartesian model.

The general idea of a foundation for knowledge can be sketched as follows. Our beliefs constitute knowledge only insofar as they are not only true, but *justified*—lucky guesses don't qualify. One claim or belief can justify another to which it is inferentially related. If one is justified in a commitment to the claim that $p$, and $q$ may be inferred from $p$, then one may for that reason be justified in a commitment to the claim that $q$. To say this is to offer a mechanism whereby justification can be inherited. But, the thought is, not *all* commitments that are justified can have inherited that status inferentially from others. There must be some other mechanism for acquiring positive justification status, to give the inheritance mechanism something to pass along. If $p_1$ inherits its status from $p_2$, and $p_2$ inherits it from $p_3$, and so on, then either

at some point a claim is repeated (some $p_n$ is identical with a $p_m$ for m < n), in which case the 'justification' is circular,

or

there never is a repetition, in which case an infinite regress arises, in which each $p_n$ has the anomalous status of an unjustified 'justifier,' which is not itself justified until an infinite number of other claims have been justified.[5]

The conclusion is that there must be some way of *being* justified without having to *be* justified. We ought to distinguish two senses of 'justification,' one indicating a status (being justified), and the other making reference to a process (justifying) that can result in possession of the status.[6] Then the conclusion is that there must be some other way of acquiring positive justificatory status besides justifying it in the sense of offering a justification. Besides inferential inheritance, there must also be some noninferential acquisition mechanism for this epistemic status.

So far, so good. Descartes concluded from this line of thought that there is a kind of claim or belief, call it a *basic* belief, that forms the foundation of all other beliefs in the sense that these beliefs are the font from which the justificatory status of all the rest flows inferentially. This does not follow, but Sellars will not contest it.[7] Descartes believed

5. This argument is obviously oversimplified in many ways. Of course justifications need not be single statements—but a corresponding dilemma occurs if sets of premises are allowed. The argument also ignores the fact that there is a regress on inferences in many ways analogous to this regress on premises, and that the two sorts of regress can interact in complex and significant ways.

6. This is an instance of what Sellars calls "the notorious 'ing'/'ed' ambiguity" [24]. (See also [[35]].)

7. See [32]. As it stands, the argument turns on an invalid quantifier inversion. What immediately follows from the foundationalist regress argument is at most that *for each* chain of justifications *there is* a belief that *is* justified (has positive justificatory status) without having to *be* justified (by appeal to another belief). It does not follow that *there is* a kind of belief such that *for each* chain of justification its terminus is a belief of that kind. A belief that stands in need of justification in one context might serve as an unjustified justifier in another. Compare: *For each* minute *there is* a woman somewhere having a baby at that time. This is true. It does *not* follow that *there is* a woman such that *for each* minute, she is having a baby at that time. If it *did* follow, then we could solve the problem of overpopulation by finding that woman and making her stop!

further that unless those beliefs were certain (the ultimate positive justificatory status), none of those inferentially based upon them could even be probable (as C. I. Lewis put it in *Mind and the World Order*). Descartes gave philosophy a decisive epistemic turn which was, at least until Kant, confused with a subjective turn. The latter is a consequence only of Descartes's peculiar and optional way of working out the former. For he defined the mind by its epistemic status, as what is best known to itself by falling within the reach of the subject's incorrigibility and local omniscience. This epistemic definition is what motivates the assimilation of events whose contents are structured like *sentences*, such as thinking that Vienna is a city in Austria, and events whose contents are structured like *pictures*, such as imagining or seeming to see a red triangle inside a green circle.

To return to the idea of using sensings of sense contents as a foundation of knowledge, then, a process is pictured something like this:

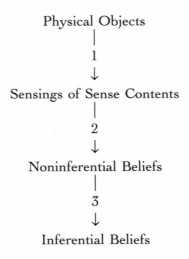

Physical Objects

|

1

↓

Sensings of Sense Contents

|

2

↓

Noninferential Beliefs

|

3

↓

Inferential Beliefs

In the standard perceptual case, it is *because* there is a red object with an octagonal facing surface in front of me that I find myself with a sensing of a red and octagonal sense content. It is *because* I have such a sense content that I acquire the noninferential belief that there is a red and octagonal object in front of me. And it is *because* I have this belief, together, perhaps, with other beliefs, that I am justified in the further inferential belief that there is a stop sign in front of me.

The point to focus on is the nature of the 'because's. The first (arrow 1) can be understood as a causal notion, perhaps the sort studied by students of the neurophysiology of perception. As such, it relates particulars describable in a nonnormative vocabulary. This is a matter-of-factual, nonepistemic relation. The final 'because' (arrow 3), on the other hand, indicates the sort of relation Sellars calls 'epistemic.' It is an inferential notion, relating sententially structured beliefs (or believables) which are repeatable abstracta — a matter of reasons rather than causes. This justificatory relation is not a natural one, but a normative one; it is not the empirical scientist, but the logician or epistemologist who has the final say about it.

The question is, what sort of relation is the middle one (arrow 2)? Does it belong in a box with the first, causal relation, or in a box with the third, inferential relation? How are the sensings of sense contents to be conceived as related to (potentially foundational) noninferential beliefs? Here is where the distinction between the epistemic and the nonepistemic, between particulars specified in the language of causes and believables specified in the language of reasons, comes into play.

Suppose that one understands the sensing of a sense content to be the existence of a nonepistemic relation between one particular, the sense content, and another, the person doing the sensing. (This is the position Sellars himself eventually endorses.) If so, then it is hard to see how the sensing of a sense content could entail or justify a claim, for instance, a noninferential belief. For only things with sentential structure can be premises of inference, not nonepistemically specified particulars. For this reason sensings, understood in terms of nonepistemic relations between sense contents and perceivers, are not well suited to serve as the ultimate ground to which inferentially inherited justification traces back. Since the occurrence of such a sensing does not entail commitment to any claim, it would be possible to have one without coming to believe anything, and certainly without coming to know anything (for this latter requires positive justificatory status). So it seems the foundationalist who wants to appeal to sensings as foundational must take the sensing of a sense content to be an epistemic fact about the sensing agent. But if so, what becomes of the particular?

*Sections 4 and 5:* The sense-datum theorist can treat sensings as epistemic noninferential beliefs, from which inferences may be made and justification status inherited, so that sensings can perform their foundational function. To retain a role for the mental particulars that are sensed (sense data, sense contents conceived as a kind of sensed object), that theorist must be willing to say the following: "The primitive notion is believing that sense content $x$ has property $F$. To sense the sense content $x$ is to believe that it has some (no matter what) characteristic $F$. The sense content, which is a particular, is the intentional object of the epistemic sensing." The important thing to notice about this analysis is that epistemic notions are presupposed, not accounted for in terms of a supposedly antecedently understood nonepistemic notion of sensing a sense content (thought of as a relation between a subject and a sense content, both of them particulars). In fact Sellars believes that no such reduction of the epistemic to the nonepistemic is possible, even in principle — though his arguments will not depend on this claim.

*Section 6:* At this point a further consideration is introduced: the ability to stand in the passive causal relations to the physical world envisaged by the fans of givenness is not something that must be *acquired* through experience or training. Organisms of the right sort get it just by being awake. But the capacity to have beliefs of the form '$x$ is $F$' involves classifying unrepeatables or particulars under repeatables or universals. It is natural to think that the capacity to classify is acquired, since one must learn by experience and training what the boundaries of the classes are. This line of thought results in the inconsistent triad of claims that the sense-datum theorist is committed to, and would like to be entitled to

A. '$S$ senses red sense content $x$,' entails '$S$ noninferentially believes (knows) that $x$ is red.'
B. The ability to sense sense contents is unacquired.
C. The capacity to have classificatory beliefs of the form '$x$ is $F$' is acquired.

If A is given up, the sensing of sense contents becomes a nonepistemic event, which can at best be a logically necessary condition of knowledge or noninferential beliefs, not a logically sufficient condition of it. To take this way out would be to discard the line pursued in [4] and [5]. If B is given up, the sense-datum theorist must either claim that we need practice to feel pain, hunger, itches, and so on when we are infants, or claim that feeling these things is not sensing. But then what is sensing? If C is given up, a story must be told about what universal concepts are innate (unacquired, inborn, wired-in) and which are not. This would require much more than even latter-day innatists such as Chomsky have claimed, since substantive concepts like *red* and *tall*, not merely grammatical forms, would have to be innate. A is the Myth of the Given, in one of its forms, and Sellars will give it up. He'll then owe (and provide) us a new account of both thoughts and sensations, and of the origins (both in the order of causation and in the order of justification) of knowledge.

*Section 7:* Sellars's diagnosis, which is not yet a treatment for the conceptual illness of givenness, is that it results from confusing two trains of thought, the first derived from an attempt to give a scientific account of perception and the acquisition of empirical information, and the second from an attempt to give a foundational epistemological account on the Cartesian model canvassed above in the discussion of [3]:

1. The idea that there are certain inner episodes — e.g., sensations of red or of C# which can occur to human beings (and brutes) without any prior process of learning or concept formation; and without which it would in some sense be impossible to see, for example, that the facing surface of a physical object is red and triangular, or hear that a certain physical sound is C#.

2. The idea that there are certain inner episodes which are the noninferential knowings that certain items are, for example, red or C#; and that these episodes are the necessary conditions of empirical knowledge as providing evidence for all other empirical propositions.

The first class consists of particulars, picked out by their causal role. The second consists of claimings structured like sentences, picked out by their inferential or justificatory role. Sellars will offer an account (starting in [45]) of the genus, *inner episode*, to which these two species belong. He will call the first kind 'sense impressions,' and the second kind 'thoughts,' and will describe the roles they play. Finally, he will explain how they are related in human knowledge. (I have talked about belief so far, where Sellars talks about knowledge, in order to emphasize that the question of the *justification* of or warrant for noninferential beliefs has yet to be discussed.)

The result of running together these two lines of thought is "the idea that a sensation of a red triangle is the very paradigm of empirical knowledge." That idea is subject to precisely those related 'perplexities' that Sellars has pointed out:

• Should we think of the sensation in question as a kind of *particular* (structured like a triangle), or as a kind of *belief* (structured like a sentence)?
• Is the capacity to have empirical knowledge like this acquired by experience, or prior to experience?
• Is it prior to the rest of our knowledge in the order of *causation*, or in the order of *justification* and evidence?

## Part II [8]-[9]
## Another Language?

*Section 8:* This and the next two sections (both marked in the original as Section 9!) are in one way an aside. The main thread is picked up again in [10]. The excursus is used to introduce some important ideas that will be discussed further along. The topic here is one possible form a sense-datum theory might take to avoid the nonepistemically-specifiable-particular vs. only-epistemically-specifiable-sententially-structured-premise dilemma Sellars is constructing for it. One might give up entirely on the nonepistemic side of things and embrace the foundational noninferential belief side. Thus Ayer sees sensing-of-sense-data talk as equivalent to and derivative from talk about how things look or seem to a subject. The suggestion comes in three parts:

a) There is a class of noninferential beliefs that form a justificatory basis for the rest of our empirical beliefs. [Note that this would be sufficient to respond to the regress argument sketched above in [[3]], though, as suggested there, it is not a necessary condition for a response.]

b) Three nested descriptions of a phenomenon. First, a platitude: I may be mistaken that there is a red triangle in front of me. It is not possible for me to be mistaken about there *seeming* to be one. Next, a reifying move: an application of the Cartesian principle that although appearance must be distinguished from reality since subjects can be in error about the latter, on pain of an infinite regress it cannot be that one might be mistaken about the former also. Finally, a foundational claim: the class mentioned in (a) consists of beliefs that would be expressed by sentences used to make perceptual reports, prefixed by a special operator "It looks to me now that . . . ," "It seems to me now that . . . ," or "It now appears to me just as though . . ."

c) Sentences of the form "S is having (or is aware of) a sense datum that is $F$" (say, red and triangular) are by definition equivalent to sentences of the form "It seems to S that he senses something $F$." On this understanding, there are no particulars that are sense data—the apparently referential singular terms that give the contrary impression must be understood contextually, like the 'it' in 'it is raining.'

*Section 9:* Here Sellars offers an observation about this approach and then formulates a dilemma for it. The observation regards merely *generic* lookings. Something can *look* polygonal without there being any determinate number of sides that it looks to have. But nothing can *be* polygonal without there being a determinate number of sides that it has. (This contrast will be explored in [17].) So the inferences one is permitted to make in sense-datum talk as introduced by the equivalence asserted by (c) are not the same as those licensed by the sense-datum theorist's talk of sense data as particulars (for which the above 'inference to further determination' goes through). Thus the code is misleading.

*Section 9 bis:* The dilemma presents a more serious objection. If sense-datum talk is just a code, it is redundant (insofar as it is not misleading). So what good is it? It can't *explain* anything about seemings or appearance. To do that it would have to be a *theory* of appearings, explaining them by relation to a certain kind of particular, namely, sense data. (Sellars begins to explain how he thinks about theoretical explanation in [21] and [22]. We then hear a lot more about this topic in the second half of the essay, beginning at [39]–[44].) But this would reintroduce the strand of thought (1) above (in

[7] and [[7]]), which the code theory is formulated precisely to avoid. The lesson is that that strand of thought is not altogether mistaken. The account Sellars will offer provides a theory of appearings, and will embrace and reconcile (1) and (2), properly understood. So (c) is not a way to avoid the problem. It allows us to look, however, at the assumptions (a) and (b) to which it was conjoined. Sellars's conclusion is that this line of thought is committed already at step (b) to the possibility of inferring from claims exclusively about how things *seem* to claims about how things actually *are*. But if, as (a) and (b) assert, all empirical evidence ultimately derives from how things seem, it is clear that such an inference cannot be warranted empirically, by inductive correlation of appearances and realities. The alternative seems to be to find a definitional reduction according to which "ordinary discourse about physical objects and perceivers could (in principle) be constructed from sentences of the form 'There looks to be a physical object with a red and triangular facing surface over there.'" Since commitment to (a) and (b) is much more widespread than commitment to (c), it is important to see what is wrong with the view the former express— why the reduction they presuppose is impossible. To that end Sellars turns to the logic of 'looks' or 'seems' talk.

## Part III [10]–[20]
## The Logic of 'Looks'

*Section 10:* To get out of the trilemma of [6], it is necessary to "examine these two ideas [(1) and (2) in [7] and [[7]]] and determine how that which survives criticism in each is properly to be combined with the other." To begin with, consider the genus inner episode to which each subject has privileged access, which is common to sensations and thoughts.

  a) Logical positivists have denied that there could be such episodes, because their existence is not intersubjectively verifiable or falsifiable. This is the source of the traditional problem of other minds, and of the inverted spectrum. To avoid entertaining such unverifiable hypotheses, one can reject idea (1).

  b) Wittgenstein and some of his followers have attacked (2), the idea that inner episodes can be premises for inferentially based knowledge, because as private they escape the net of public discourse and language learning (the beetle in the box, and the private language argument).

Sellars disagrees with both of these. We'll return to the first later under the heading 'behaviorism' ([54]–[55]). What one should reject in order to avoid the problem of other minds and the possibility of inverted spectra is the Myth of the Given, not the notion of inner episodes. Sellars will argue (in [45]–[47]) that (b) is both too strong and too weak. It is too strong in that inner episodes need not escape the net of public discourse. The second half of *EPM* has the task of showing us how to think of inner episodes — as theoretical entities that became observable. It is too weak in that this repudiation of inner episodes is not (as we see in the following sections) sufficient to avoid Sellars's foe, the Myth of the Given.

*Section 11:* The problem is that noninferential beliefs of the form "*X* looks *F* to *S*" can be held to be given in the bad sense even if, for inverted spectrum and beetle-in-a-box reasons, one refuses to talk about intrinsic properties of these lookings. That is, even if one does not assume (as one ought not, see [21]) that if anything *looks* F to S, something *is* F (the "sense-datum inference"), one can still fall prey to the Myth. In order to attack this more insidious form of the Myth, then, Sellars considers the notion of 'looks' talk independent of any relation it might be taken to have to inner episodes as particulars.

*Section 12:* The question is, Does *looks-red* come before *is-red* conceptually (and so in the order of explanation)? That is, could the latter be defined in terms of the former in such a way that one could learn how to use the defining concept *(looking-F)* first, and only afterwards, by means of the definition, learn how to use the defined concept *(is-F)?* Descartes and his tradition claimed that *looks-F* talk, with which it is possible to form a class of statements about which subjects are incorrigible, is a foundation of knowledge, and so must be prior in this sense to *is-F* talk, with which it is possible to express only corrigible, inferred beliefs. This view is the essence of Descartes's foundationalism.

Descartes was struck by the fact that the appearance/reality distinction seems not to apply to appearances. While I may be mistaken about whether something *is* red (or whether the tower, in the distance, *is* square), I cannot in the same way be mistaken about whether it *looks* red to me now.[8] While I may legitimately be challenged by a doubter — "Perhaps the item is not *really* red; perhaps it only *seems* red" —

---

8. I might be mistaken about whether *red* is what it looks, that is, whether the property expressed by the word 'red' is the one it looks to have. But that, the thought goes, is another matter. I cannot be mistaken that it looks that way, like *that*, where this latter phrase is understood as having a noncomparative use. It *looks-red*, i.e., it has a distinctive phenomenal property, which we may inconveniently only happen to be able to pick out by its association with a word for a real-world property.

there is no room for the further doubt, "Perhaps the item does not even *seem* red; perhaps it only *seems* to seem red." If it seems to seem red, then it really does seem red. The *looks, seems,* or *appears* operators collapse if we try to iterate them. A contrast between appearance and reality is marked by the distinction between *looks-F* and *F* for ordinary (reality-indicating) predicates 'F'. But no corresponding contrast is marked by the distinction between *looks-to-look-F* and *looks-F*. Appearances are reified by Descartes as things that really are just however they appear. He inferred that we do not know them mediately, by means of representings that introduce the possibility of *mis*-representing (a distinction between how they really are and how they merely appear, i.e., are represented as being). Rather, we know them *immediately*—simply by having them. Thus appearings—thought of as a realm of entities *reported* on by noninferentially elicited claims about how things *look* (for the visual case), or more generally *seem,* or *appear*—show up as having the ideal qualifications for epistemologically secure foundations of knowledge: we cannot make mistakes about them. Just *having* an appearance ("being appeared-to F-ly," in one of the variations Sellars discusses) counts as *knowing* something: not that something is *F,* to be sure, but at least that something *looks-, seems-,* or *appears-F.* The possibility accordingly arises of reconstructing our knowledge by starting out only with knowledge of this sort—knowledge of how things look, seem, or appear—and building up in some way to our knowledge (if any) of how things really are (outside the realm of appearance).

This project requires that concepts of the form *looks-F* be intelligible in principle in advance of grasping the corresponding concepts *F* (or *is-F*). Sellars is a linguistic pragmatist about the conceptual order; that is, for him, grasp of a concept just is mastery of the use of a word.⁹ So he systematically pursues the methodology of translating questions of conceptual priority into questions about the relative autonomy of various language games. He will argue that in this case, Descartes got things backwards. 'Looks' talk does not form an autonomous stratum of the language—it is not a language-game one could play though one played no other. One must already be able to use 'is-*F*' talk in order to master 'looks-*F*' talk, which turns out to be parasitic on it. In this precise practical sense, *is-F* is *conceptually* (Sellars often says 'logically') *prior* to *looks-F.*

*Section 13:* The definition being considered for exploitation in a Cartesian order of explanation (and so, ultimately, of justification) is

$$x \text{ } is \text{ red} = _{df.} x \text{ would } look \text{ red under standard conditions.}$$

Sellars will show how to acknowledge that this claim is definitionally true without countenancing the conceptual priority of 'looks' talk, and hence without giving aid and comfort to givenness and the sort of foundationalism it supports.

*Section 14:* Sentences can have reporting (noninferential) uses as well as (merely) fact stating (inferential) uses.¹⁰ For reliable reporters, one may infer from the fact that one is dis-

9. For it to be a *concept* one grasps thereby, the word must have an inferential role; it must be usable in formulating premises and conclusions of inferences assessable as correct or incorrect. Thus acquiring the differential responsive dispositions required to use the word 'ouch' does not qualify as grasping a concept. See [[16]] below.

10. Sellars's terminology is strained here. There is no reason to deny that noninferential reports are in the fact-stating line of work, and so, when true, state facts. The preferred usage is to see the distinction between claims that are noninferentially elicited and those that arise as the conclusions of inferences as a distinction *within* fact-stating discourse.

posed to say that $x$ is $F$ and that the conditions are as far as one knows standard and that when under those conditions one is so disposed it is usually the case that $x$ is $F$, to the conclusion that $x$ is in fact $F$. (The reporter's having to believe all of this, and so to understand it, is crucial to Sellars's later argument). Understanding the possibility of systematic error in the responsive dispositions of reporters introduces a new dimension in the relation between practices of *reporting* and those of *inferring*. Here Sellars introduces the illustrative parable of young John in the tie shop.

*Section 15:* Where collateral beliefs indicate that systematic error is likely, the subject learns not to make the report '$x$ is $F$,' to which his previously inculcated responsive dispositions incline him, but to make a new kind of claim: '$x$ *looks* (or seems) $F$.' Of course it is tempting to take this as a new kind of report, indeed, a report of a special kind of particular, a sense datum. This report, then, is naturally thought of as reporting a minimal, noninferentially ascertainable, foundationally basic fact, about which each subject is incorrigible. There are two points here which might be distinguished. First, it is a mistake in any case to treat what is reported as foundationally basic facts, for the concepts needed to formulate them turn out to depend on other concepts, which are not formed using any analogue of a 'looks'-operator. (See [32].) Second, it is a mistake to treat these as reports at all—since they *evince* a disposition to call something $F$, but may not happily be thought of as *saying that* one has such a disposition. Sellars wavers on the second point, but he is firm on the first.

*Section(s) 16:* Sellars's alternative analysis depends on distinguishing two different dimensions of the use of a noninferential report. First, each report is the manifestation of some *reliable differential responsive disposition.* That is, it is the result of one's being trained to behave in a certain way when in certain environmental situations (like a pigeon trained to peck at the red square when the red light comes on). What is the difference between a parrot trained to utter "That's red!" when and only when confronted by the visible presence of something red, and a genuine noninferential reporter of the same circumstance? Having the differential responsive dispositions is not enough to have the concept, else a chunk of iron that rusts in wet environments and not in dry ones would have to be counted as having the concepts of wet and dry environments. What more, besides the parrot's *sentience,* is required for the *sapience* that consists in responding differentially by applying a *concept?* Sellars's answer, invoking the second dimension of reporting, is that the response must be taking up a position in the space of reasons—making a move in the game of giving and asking for reasons. The genuine noninferential reporter of red things has, and the parrot has not, mastered the *inferential role* played by reports of that type—where inferential role is a matter of what conclusions one is entitled to draw from such a statement when it is overheard, what would count as a reason for it, and what is incompatible with it and so a reason against it. This is a matter of the inferentially articulated content of the assertional commitment undertaken by the reporter in virtue of the performance that is the reporting: what the reporter is responsible for. Sellars's term for this second dimension is *endorsement,* a matter of what one is linguistically *committed* to (the inferential consequences of one's claims) or responsible for (how it could be justified) in virtue of one's assertional performance. This notion of *responsibility,* or of what conclusions one has given others the *right* to draw, or has *obliged* oneself to draw, and what other commitments would count as *entitling* one to the commitment one has undertaken is the normative element in linguistic conduct, whose irreducibility to descriptive aspects (such as responsive dispositions) lies at the base of the epistemic/nonepistemic distinction, and is the source of Sellars's remark about the naturalistic fallacy at the end of [5].

On Sellars's understanding, the ability to use '*x* looks green' correctly appeals to the same responsive dispositions acquired in learning to use '*x* is green' correctly. But these two sorts of remarks elicited in accordance with those dispositions support quite different inferences. In particular, the parable of the tie shop shows that in saying that something merely *looks* green, one can be understood to be doing two things: expressing one's noninferential differential responsive disposition to call it green (to commit oneself to the claim that it is green, with all of its inferential consequences and justificatory obligations), and at the same time explicitly *withholding* one's endorsement of that claim. For collateral beliefs concerning the possibility of systematic error under the prevailing circumstances of observation have undermined the reporter's confidence in his reliability—that is, in the correctness of the inference from "X is disposed noninferentially to report the presence of something green (seen by electric lighting)," to "There is (probably) something green there."

This analysis of what one is doing in using 'looks' explains the incorrigibility of 'looks' talk. One can be wrong about whether something *is* green because the claim one endorses, the commitment one undertakes, may turn out to be incorrect. For instance, its inferential consequences may be incompatible with other facts one is or comes to be in a position to know independently. But in saying that something *looks* green, one is not endorsing a claim, but *withholding* endorsement from one. Such a reporter is merely evincing a disposition to do something that for other reasons (e.g., suspicion that the circumstances of observation lead to systematic error) he is unwilling to do—namely, endorse a claim. Such a reporter cannot be wrong, because he has held back from making a commitment. This is why the *looks, seems,* and *appears* operators do not iterate. Their function is to express the withholding of endorsement from the sentence that appears within the scope of the operator. There is no sensible contrast between 'looks-to-look *F*' and 'looks-*F*,' of the sort there is between 'looks-*F*' and '(is-)*F*' because the first 'looks' has already withheld endorsement from the only content in the vicinity to which one might be committed (to something's being *F*). There is no further withholding work for the second 'looks' to do. There is nothing left to take back. Since asserting 'X looks *F*' is not undertaking a propositionally contentful commitment—but only expressing an overrideable disposition to do so—there is no issue as to whether or not that commitment (which one?) is correct.

Sellars accordingly explains the incorrigibility of appearance-claims, which had so impressed Descartes. He does so in terms of the practices of using words, which are what grasp of the relevant appearance concepts must amount to, according to his methodological linguistic pragmatism. But once we have seen the source and nature of this incorrigibility—in down-to-earth, practical, resolutely nonmetaphysical terms—we see also why it is precisely unsuited to use as an epistemological foundation for the rest of our (risky, corrigible) empirical knowledge. For, first, the incorrigibility of claims about how things merely *look* simply reflects their emptiness: the fact that they are not really claims at all. And second, the same story shows us that 'looks' talk is not an autonomous language game — one that could be played though one played no other. It is entirely parasitic on the practice of making risky empirical reports of how things actually are. Thus Descartes seized on a genuine phenomenon — the incorrigibility of claims about appearances, reflecting the non-iterability of operators like *looks*, *seems*, and *appears* — but misunderstood its nature, and so mistakenly thought it available to play an epistemologically foundational role for which it is in no way suited.

This analysis of "the logic of 'looks' talk," along with the consequent diagnosis of the errors of a foundationalism based on the incorrigibility of our epistemic access to appearances, is the constructive core of Sellars's critique of Cartesianism. It does not purport to be a knock-down argument; for it can only be as persuasive as its account of how 'looks' talk works, and alternatives are always possible.[11] What it is meant to do

11. "There are many interesting and subtle questions about the dialectics of 'looks'-talk, into which I do not have space to enter" [17]. Sellars focuses on one sort of use that 'looks' has: first-person, noninferential uses. But as he points out in this section, 'looks' also has third-person, (merely) fact-stating uses, as when S' says: "X looks *F* to S." The account generalizes to these cases straightforwardly. In making this claim, S' is doing two things: attributing to S a disposition noninferentially to report that X is *F*, and herself withholding endorsement from the claim that X is *F*. The words used to make this report do not settle whether S' would attribute to S the endorsement, or the withholding of endorsement, from the claim that X is *F* (that is, whether S' takes it that the disposition being she attributes to S issues in an endorsement, or is overridden and withheld by S). More expressively powerful and discriminating regimented uses that do mark such distinctions are easily contrived. (This same idea will account for the nontrivial iterated or embedded uses of 'looks' or 'seems' made possible by shifts of perspective: "It seems to S' that X looks *F* to S," and so on.)

Further uses of 'looks' that are more challenging to the Sellarsian account have been pointed out by Joe Camp. These are cases where we use 'looks *F*' without a

is to remove the temptation to go the Cartesian foundationalist route, by explaining, without explaining away, the exact
nature of that temptation.

*Section 17:* (This line of thought is completed in [22]). We
begin to look for some confirmation of the two-pronged
account of 'looks' talk as expressing a differential responsive
disposition to make a specified noninferential report, while
withholding endorsement of that claim. The confirmation
takes the form of explanations of otherwise puzzling features
of appearance-talk. Consider the three sentences:

(i)   The apple over there is red.
(ii)  The apple over there looks red.
(iii) It looks as though there were a red apple over there.

Utterances of these sentences can express the same responsive disposition to report the presence of a red apple, but
they endorse (take responsibility for the inferential consequences of) different parts of that claim. (i) endorses both
the existence of the apple and its quality of redness. (ii)
endorses only the existence of the apple. The 'looks' locution
explicitly cancels the qualitative commitment or endorsement. (iii) explicitly cancels both the existential and the

corresponding practice of using the unmodified '(is) *F*.' Thus after the optometrist
puts pupil-dilating drops in my eyes, I may say, "Things look blurry." 'Blurry' does
not express a way things could *be*. It is essentially an expression pertaining to images
or representations. Taking this sort of use of 'looks' as central and paradigmatic
could encourage the reintroduction of the idea that noninferential uses of 'looks'
are genuine reports, reports of intrinsic features of appearances as such. Sellarsians
will presumably see these 'intrinsic' uses of 'looks' rather as sophisticated late-com-
ing possibilities, derivative from the central uses, and to be explained in terms of
them. Sellars himself never discusses this issue.

In a note to the 1963 edition, Sellars suggests that one might distinguish between
'looks *F*' and 'looks to be *F*,' in a way that corresponds to Chisholm's distinction
between noncomparative and comparative 'appears' statements.

qualitative endorsements. Thus, if someone claims that there is in fact no apple over there, he is asserting something incompatible with (i) and (ii), but not with (iii). If he denies that there is anything red over there, he asserts something incompatible with (i), but not with (ii) or (iii). Sellars's account of the practice of using 'looks,' in terms of the withholding of endorsement when one suspects systematic error in one's responsive dispositions, can account for the difference in scope of endorsement that (i)–(iii) exhibit. But how could that difference be accounted for on a sense-datum approach?

In this section Sellars points out another virtue of his account, as opposed to sense-datum theories, namely, the possibility of reporting a merely *generic* (more accurately, merely determinable) look. (Recall that Sellars introduced this phenomenon already in [9].) Thus it is possible for an apple to look red, without its looking any specific shade of red (crimson, scarlet, etc.). It is possible for a plane figure to look many-sided without there being some particular number of sides (say 119) which it looks to have. But if 'looks' statements are to be understood as reports of the presence before the eye of the mind of a particular which *is F,* how can this possibility be understood? Particulars are completely determinate. A horse has a particular number of hairs, though as Sellars points out, it can *look* to have merely 'a lot' of them. It is a particular shade of brown (or several shades), even though it may look only darkly colored. So how are such generic, merely determinable, looks possible? Sellars's account is in terms of scope of endorsement. One says that the plane figure looks 'many-sided' instead of '119-sided' just in case one is willing only to endorse (be held responsible for justifying) the more general claim. This is a matter of how far one is willing to trust one's responsive dispositions, a matter of the epistemic credence one feels they deserve or are able to sustain. Particulars, even if they are sense contents, cannot be colored without being some determinate color and shade. How then can the sense-datum theorist — who wants to say that when something *looks* F to S, something in S *is* F — account for the fact that something can look colored without looking to be any particular color, or look red without looking to be any particular shade of red? So Sellars's account of 'looks' talk in terms of endorsement can account for two aspects of that kind of discourse that no theory that invokes a given can explain: the scope distinctions between qualitative and existential lookings, and the possibility of merely generic or determinable lookings.

*Section 18:* On this account, then, one must first acquire the practice of reporting red objects (getting both the appropriate responsive dispositions and an understanding of what one is endorsing by making such a claim), and only then can one learn to make reports expressing those same dispositions, but which are more guarded in their endorsement. As the argument of the previous section has shown, the mastery of different endorsements required can be quite sophisticated. One may, for instance, discriminate existential and qualitative lookings, and various grades of determinability. Thus to know when something *looks* red, one must understand what it is to *be* red, and a good deal besides.[12] We can see at this point that the sentence we worried about in [13] is true

12. In a footnote added to the 1963 reprinting of the essay, Sellars points out that his story is compatible with distinguishing a *rudimentary* concept corresponding to the use of 'green,' which one can have *without* having mastered the use of 'looks green,' and a *richer* concept (corresponding more closely to ours) which is achieved only once one has also mastered 'looks' talk. This observation opens the door to distinguishing (as McDowell does) concepts corresponding to *secondary qualities* as those mastery of which requires mastery of the associated 'looks' vocabulary—as, arguably, *green* does, while *massive*, and perhaps *square*, do not.

because it is a definition, not of *is-red*, but of *standard conditions*. For standard conditions are just those in which one's responsive dispositions can be trusted, and ought to be fully endorsed. Given such a definition, one can investigate empirically what those conditions are.

*Sections 19 and 20:* These sections return to the question of the acquisition of various capacities involved in mastering an observation concept, the question that set up the trilemma of [6]. We now know that these capacities involve both regular responsive dispositions and a capacity to manipulate endorsements inferentially, a nonepistemic and an epistemic skill respectively. The specifically *inferential* articulation required for endorsements to qualify as *conceptually* contentful introduces at least a limited *holism* into Sellars's picture: one could not have one concept unless one had many others to which it is inferentially related: "The essential point is that even to have the more rudimentary concept [of *green*, say] presupposes having a battery of other concepts." This entails rejecting the idea that "fundamental concepts pertaining to observable fact have that logical independence of one another which is characteristic of the empiricist tradition." These sections do not present Sellars's argument in a perspicuous, or even linear, fashion, and the argument is repeated in more satisfactory form at [33]–[37], where we will discuss it.

## Part IV [21]–[23]
## Explaining Looks

*Sections 21 and 22:* [17] discussed the issue of the scope of endorsement, which is treated in the third paragraph of [21]. Sellars reformulates that account in terms of the events that are lookings and seeings, where earlier we discussed the reports causally occasioned by those events. The first two paragraphs of [22] and the third paragraph of [21] then present a preliminary account of a distinction between two ways in which some phenomenon can be explained:

(i) By deducing it from some empirical generalization formulated entirely in terms of observables (things that can be noninferentially reported). Explaining a change in pressure of a gas sample by appealing to the law PV = kT, together with suitable background conditions, is an example.

(ii) By postulating unobservable entities, and subsuming the phenomenon under laws involving those theoretical entities. Explaining the change in pressure of a gas by appealing to the kinetic theory of gases and its postulated molecules and their interactions is an example.

Once again, this discussion is really out of place here, serving merely as a dark foreshadowing of a line of argument that will be pursued in more detail later (beginning at [39]–[44]). Sellars does here raise the important question that remains even after we have understood existential, qualitative, and unqualified 'looks' statements in terms of scope of endorsement (as in [17]), namely, what is it that is common to the three cases? The answer, we will see, is "sense impressions of red." But that is an answer we will not be able to understand until the very end of the essay ([62]).

*Section 23:* This section discusses the question of what things can literally be red. Sellars's claim is that only physical objects can, and that it is a mistake to think that even facing surfaces can, except in a derivative sense. The discussion as it stands is unsatisfactory, since criteria of primacy of sense and literalness of attribution are not forthcoming. Once again, a later discussion is being prefigured, in this case concerning the 'of-red'ness of sensations in [60]–[61].

Parts V and VI (Sections [24]–[29]) offer a discussion of the British Empiricists' treatment of impressions. They fill in some of the historical background of Sellars's discussion, but are not central or essential to the development of his argument.

## Part V [24]–[25]
## Impressions and Ideas: A Logical Point

*Sections 24 and 25:* A discussion of the intentionality of 'sensation of . . .' Sellars's view is that Descartes mistakenly assimilated sensations and thoughts because of the way in which each is 'of' or 'about' or directed at something. There need be no red triangle for me to have a sensation 'of' one, and there need be no golden mountain for me to have a thought 'of' one. But this is a superficial similarity, for the kind of aboutness is in fact quite different in the two cases. An equally important motivation for the assimilation, which Sellars does not mention here, is the incorrigibility and transparency, the epistemic privilege accorded to reports of sensations and of thoughts. Here Sellars points out "the notorious 'ing'/'ed' ambiguity" as it applies to the concept of *experience.*

## Part VI [26]–[29]
## Impressions and Ideas: A Historical Point

*Section 26:* The inverted spectrum problem cannot be stated without recourse to some version of the Myth of the Given.

❈     ❈     ❈

*Section 27:* A central epistemological problem of the empiricists Locke, Berkeley, and Hume is taken to be the question how, given that we can be aware of completely *determinate* sense repeatables, we can come to be aware also of *determinable* sense repeatables. Determinate/determinable is like species/genus, except that there is no separately specifiable differentiating factor. Colors are the prime example: scarlet is a more determinate shade of the determinable color red, as red is a determination of the determinable colored.

*Section 28:* The British Empiricists ". . . all take for granted that the human mind has an innate ability to be aware of certain determinate sorts — indeed, that we are aware of them simply by virtue of having sensations and images." That is, they did not ask a corresponding question about how, given that we can be aware of particular unrepeatable *token* sense contents, we can come to be aware also of their repeatable *types*, even maximally determinate ones.

*Section 29:* Against this Sellars will argue for what he calls 'psychological nominalism' (not the best imaginable name), according to which all awareness of repeatables (whether determinate or determinable) is a linguistic affair, and hence may not be presupposed in one's account of the acquisition and functioning of language. Sellars is proposing a linguistic, social theory of awareness. He has in mind more by this term than simply being awake (not being asleep): he is after awareness in the sense of *sapience,* not of *sentience.* It is classificatory awareness, awareness of something as something. But not all acts of classification are acts of awareness. As pointed out above in [[16]], anything with stable dispositions to respond differentially to stimuli can be thought of as classifying the stimuli according to the repeatable responses those stimuli elicit. A parrot trained to respond differentially to red things in its environment does not display the sort of awareness that Sellars is explaining. Such awareness, specifically *conceptual* awareness, requires something beyond being awake and classifying by differential response.

## Part VII [30]–[31]
## The Logic of 'Means'

*Section 30:* Anyone whose account of the prelinguistic awareness that makes language acquisition possible assigns it an inferential structure (Sellars says 'logical,' but that is just 1950s talk for 'conceptual,' which for Sellars can be parsed as 'inferential') and is committed to the Myth of the Given. Such conceptual awareness involves not only classification, but making the classifications significant in inferences. It is at this point that statements of fact are made, particulars referred to and classified under universals. On the sort of account Sellars opposes to the Myth, conceptual content is inferentially articulated. But inference is a process arising only within the "game of giving and asking for reasons," which essentially involves beliefs. This is a normative realm, of commitment and entitlement to claims, of endorsement and justification. It is what Sellars has been calling the 'epistemic.' The Myth is to think that anything could intrinsically, naturally, or necessarily possess a particular significance for this realm, independent of the acquisition or deployment of concepts by the one for whom it has that significance. Acts of awareness as traditionally conceived, as entailing the existence of something sufficiently belief-like to serve as the ultimate inferential ground of empirical knowledge (never mind as themselves constituting knowledge), would have to have just such a property.

*Section 31:* So learning a meaning ought not to be understood as associating something one is already aware of with a verbal symbol. But isn't this the natural way to understand statements like "'Rot' (in German) means red"? How else can Sellars understand this sentence except as expressing an association between one's awareness of the determinable repeatable quality and the word 'rot'? His answer is that meaning claims like this really assert that the mentioned expression ('rot') plays the same conceptual functional role as the used expression ('red'). "These considerations make it clear that nothing whatever can be inferred . . . about the exact way in which the word 'red' is related to red things, from the truth of the semantical statement "'red" means the quality *red.*'"

## Part VIII [32]–[38]
## Does Empirical Knowledge Have a Foundation?

*Section 32:* Another incorrect, foundationalist account is described here. Sellars disagrees with only one bit of this story, though it turns out to be an important bit. Foundationalism is the claim that there is a structure of particular beliefs such that

(1) Each one is noninferentially arrived at.
(2) The beliefs in (1) presuppose no other belief, either particular or general.
(3) These noninferentially acquired beliefs constitute the ultimate court of appeal for all factual claims.

Sellars accepts (1) and (3), but denies (2). His project at this point is to show how a bit of knowledge (belief) can, and indeed how all of it does, presuppose other knowledge (belief), even though it is not inferred from that other knowledge or belief. This possibility was not seriously examined by the classical epistemological tradition. It is a certain hierarchical picture of *understanding* (at this level a necessary condition of believing) that Sellars rejects. He does not object to a hierarchical picture of *justification,* once that has been suitably disentangled from bad foundationalism concerning the nature and acquisition of belief.

For Sellars, there is no such thing as a noninferential belief, if by that one means a belief one could have without grasping its inferential connection to at least some other beliefs. For to understand a sentence, to grasp a propositional content (a necessary condition of having a belief) is to place it in the space of reasons, to assign it an inferential role in the game of giving and asking for reasons, as entailing some other contents and being incompatible with others. A noninferential report or belief can properly be called 'noninferential' only in the sense that the reporter's commitment to an essentially inferentially articulated content is elicited noninferentially on this occasion—that is, that it is elicited as a response to some nonlinguistic, nonepistemic environing circumstance, rather than as a response to another belief or assertion. Noninferential beliefs do not form an autonomous discursive stratum: there could be no language game consisting entirely of noninferential reports. (Notice that this is a stronger claim than that made above in connection with 'looks'-talk. For this claim concerns *any* kind of noninferential report, whether what they report is inner or outer, appearances or empirical realities.) For any sentence to have noninferential uses, some sentences must have inferential ones. For the conceptual content expressed by a sentence (what is believe*d*) essentially involves its potential as a premise and as a conclusion of inferences. Unless one can employ noninferentially acquired beliefs as the premises of inferences leading to further beliefs, their acquisition does not qualify as acquiring *beliefs* (something propositionally contentful) at all. On this inferentialist picture of conceptual content, one cannot have one concept without having many inferentially interrelated ones. This does not mean that there could not be a language consisting only of expressions for observables, however. For the concepts of observables are concepts that have noninferential, reporting, uses. The requirement is only that the concepts that can be used to make noninferential reports must also be available to be applied inferentially, as the conclusions of inferences whose premises are the noninferential applications of other concepts.

Sellars begins by asking about the nature of the *authority* (a patently normative notion) of noninferential beliefs, that is, their capacity to justify other claims. A distinction is needed first between sentence *types* and sentence *tokens*: the type is repeatable and can be instantiated on different occasions, whereas the token is unrepeatable. It is the utterance or inscription of the sentence on a particular occasion. So if the distinction is applied to letters instead of sentences, the sequence 'aeaaeea' contains two letter types and seven letter tokens, four of one type and three of the other. Now it can be seen that it is sentence tokens whose justification is at issue. For though there are some sentences that are justified, if they are justified at all, whenever they are tokened, such as '2 + 2 = 4,' and 'Red is a color,' there are others that can be justified (and true) on one occasion and not justified or true on another. Then only the tokens and not the types can be said to be justified. These are sentences like 'That car is red,' or 'I'm hungry now,' which contain words whose reference is determined by the actual circumstances in which the sentence is tokened. These are called "token reflexive" expressions. Many, though not all, of the noninferential beliefs putatively described in (1)–(3) above are token reflexive. Authority or credibility (positive justification status) is either extrinsic, coming from something else, in this case by inferential inheritance, or intrinsic. Intrinsic credibility may be associated with types, as in meaning-analytic statements such as 'All bachelors are unmarried males,' or with tokens, as in 'This is red' (or, given Sellars's account of 'looks,' 'This looks red').

*Section 33:* Sellars now considers a line of thought according to which intrinsically credible types and intrinsically credible tokens, analytic claims[13] and observation reports, are similar in that they are both types such that their being *correctly* tokened, that is, tokened according to the *rules* for the use of all the component expressions, is a sufficient, not just a necessary, condition of their being true and justified (hence not just believed but known). Sellars can swallow all of this

---

13. In "Two Dogmas of Empiricism" Quine objects to the notion of meaning-analytic claims (claims true in virtue solely of the meanings of their words) on the broadly pragmatist grounds that there is no practically discernible status corresponding to this supposed category. Claims taken to be analytic, such as "All bachelors are unmarried males," are not immune from revision, known a priori, or otherwise distinguished from statements of very general fact, such as "There have been black dogs." Sellars accepts analyticity, which he associates with the practical status of counterfactual robustness. This line of thought ties our concepts to what we take to be laws of nature. (See Sellars's "Concepts as Involving Laws, and Inconceivable without Them," in *Pure Pragmatics and Possible Worlds,* and "Counterfactuals, Dispositions, and the Causal Modalities," in *Minnesota Studies in the Philosophy of Science,* ed. Herbert Feigl, Michael Scriven, and Grover Maxwell, vol. 2, pp. 225–308 [Minneapolis: University of Minnesota Press, 1958].) So conceived, analytic claims are neither immune from revision nor known a priori.

except the bit about rules. The idea that he will reject is that analytic statements are true by virtue of discursive definition (definition of a linguistic expression in terms of other linguistic expressions), while observation reports are true by virtue of ostensive definitions. Ostensive definitions are the only sort we can give of terms like 'red.' They consist of defining the expression by exhibiting samples of the things it applies to (pointing to red objects). The usual foundationalist infinite regress argument can be applied to show that not all expressions of the language can be discursively defined on pain of circularity or infinite regress (in either case no definition is achieved). So there must be ostensive definitions in the language. These definitions, just like the discursive ones, codify the rules of appropriate usage of the expressions they define. Just as following those rules is sufficient for the truth of analytic statements, so following the 'rules' of ostensive definition is to be sufficient for the truth of observation reports. (Such a rule might look like the definition in [13].) At this point Sellars disagrees. One can imagine following the rules for the use of 'this,' 'is,' and 'green' only if one has some idea of prelinguistic awareness of green—the Myth. For Sellars it is incoherent to talk of ostensive definitions setting up rules for using 'green,' for there is no language available in which such rules could be stated. Ostensive definitions establish practices; they are regular, but not rule governed.[14]

*Section 34:* The notion that the authority of noninferential reports rests on episodes of nonverbal, hence *nonconceptual,*

14. This distinction, and the need for some sense in which a practice (paradigmatically, a linguistic practice) can be governed by norms even though its practitioners cannot be said to be following rules, are Sellars's topic in his important essay "Some Reflections on Language Games," reprinted in *Science, Perception, and Reality* (London: Routledge & Kegan Paul, Ltd., 1963).

awareness, which verbal performances express, is a version of the Myth. From Sellars's point of view, such episodes are the tortoise underneath the elephant.

*Section 35:* Here Sellars presents his alternative view. It begins with the observation that ". . . a token of 'This is green' in the presence of a green item . . . expresses observational knowledge [only if] it is a manifestation of a tendency to produce tokens of 'This is green'—given a certain 'set' (context of collateral commitments and circumstances) if and only if a green object is being looked at in standard conditions. . . ." That is, it must be the expression of a reliable differential responsive disposition. But photocells and parrots could satisfy this condition, which shows that so far only the responsive dispositions part of the observation report has been specified. It remains to add conditions to capture the epistemic side, the dimension of endorsement, of undertaking inferentially articulated commitments, of producing a performance with a distinctive kind of authority.

To have the authority of knowledge, the report must not only *be* reliable; it must be *taken to be* reliable. In fact Sellars claims that it must be *known* by the reporter to be reliable (and in this he perhaps goes too far): ". . . the perceiver must know that tokens of 'This is green' are symptoms of the presence of green objects in conditions which are standard for visual perception." 'Justification' has the 'ing/ed' ambiguity (cf. [24]): justifying, a practical activity, or being justified, a normative status. Sellars claims that one cannot have the status except when it is possible to redeem that claim to authority and epistemic privilege by engaging in the activity of justifying it. This claim of the priority of practice over status is a specific variety of pragmatism, to which Sellars adheres. The difference between a noninferential reporter and a photocell, or a parrot trained to utter 'It's getting warmer' as the temperature rises, does not lie in the reliability or range of their responsive dispositions. It lies in the capacity of the reporter to redeem the commitment undertaken, the authority claimed by the reporting, by justifying the claim (if challenged) by giving reasons for it. The by now familiar basic point is that in order to count as making a claim (expressing a belief) at all, the reporter must be "in the space of giving and asking for reasons," in addition to having the right responsive dispositions. The further claim being forwarded here is that for a noninferential report to express knowledge (or the belief it expresses to constitute knowledge), the reporter must be able to justify it, by exhibiting reasons for it. This is to say that the reporter must be able to exhibit it as the conclusion of an inference, even though that is not how the commitment originally came about.

The inference in question is what might be called a "reliability inference." One justifies a noninferentially elicited report that something is red by noting that one was disposed noninferentially to apply the concept *red* to it, and pointing out that one is a reliable reporter of red things in these circumstances. To say that one is reliable is just to say that the inference from one's being disposed to call something red to its actually being red is a good one. Thus the reliability of one's differential responsive dispositions, together with the report's being an exercise of those dispositions, justifies—offers good reasons for—the report. In insisting that in order properly to be credited with knowledge a reporter must be able to offer an inferential justification of the belief in question, Sellars is endorsing an epistemological internalism that puts him at odds with more recent reliabilist externalists in epistemology. Their claim is that the real function of the traditional justification condition on knowledge is to rule out *accidentally* true beliefs. If so, then the rationale for engaging in assessments of whether various beliefs qualify as knowledge is perfectly well-served by insisting only that candidate beliefs result from reliable belief-forming mechanisms—that is, mechanisms that are likely to lead to truths, whether or not the reporter knows that they are. Forming beliefs that one can justify then appears as one reliable mechanism among others.

Of course, from Sellars's point of view it would be a mistake to conclude from this line of thought that one could trade inferential justification for reliable belief-formation in a wholesale fashion. For that it is *beliefs* that one is forming, that what one is doing is applying *concepts*, is a matter of their specifically *inferential* articulation—their role in the game of giving and asking for reasons, justifying and demanding justifications. Against that background of inferential practice, however, it is not obvious why Sellars should resist the reliabilist's suggestion. Why isn't it enough that the *attributor* of knowledge know that the reporter is reliable, that the *attributor* of knowledge endorse the inference from the reporter's responsive disposition noninferentially to apply the concept *red* to the thing's (probably) being red? Why should the reporter herself have to be able to offer the inferential justification for her noninferential report? (This is the thought behind the qualification offered parenthetically early in the second paragraph above.)

*Section 36:* The moral is that on the true view "one could not have observational knowledge of any fact unless one knew many other things as well." This is not to say that observation reports are somehow results of inferences after all, but only that, though noninferential, they must be justifiable to be justified. The false view thinks it is supposed to give a causal description of how knowledge is possessed, but "... in characterizing an episode or state as that of knowing we are not giving an empirical description of that episode or state: we are placing it in the logical space of reasons, or justifying and being able to justify what one says." Thus everything irrelevant to justification, either to knowing what would be a justification or to being entitled to produce one, is a noncognitive causal antecedent, perhaps a necessary condition of empirical knowledge, but not one that is constitutive of it. Nor is the general point specific to the normative, epistemic status of knowledge—though Sellars does not point this out. He could as well have said that in characterizing an episode or state as one of *believing,* or *applying concepts,* or *grasping propositional contents* we are not giving an empirical description of that episode or state but placing it in the logical space of reasons, or justifying and being able to justify what one says. For only what is inferentially articulated is conceptually contentful (and hence qualifies as a believable or claimable) at all. As we saw in the previous section, however, Sellars does want to insist further that one cannot *know* noninferentially that something is green unless one also *knows* that one is a reliable reporter of green things under the prevailing circumstances.

*Section 37:* This view—the one Sellars endorses—seems to involve an infinite regress. For how could we have acquired knowledge that tokens of 'This is green' are reliable symptoms ... unless we had had knowledge of such facts as 'This is green,' and "This is a token of 'this is green'" beforehand?[15]

---

15. Notice that this is a problem Sellars need not have faced, had he endorsed the modified externalism offered to him in [[35]] above.

Sellars's answer is that we can acquire knowledge of facts of these three types simultaneously, but that we can know facts that bear on events that occurred before we acquired any of this knowledge. Thus: ". . . it requires only that it is correct to say that Jones now knows, thus remembers, that these particular facts did obtain. It does not require that it be correct to say that at the time these facts did obtain he then knew them to obtain. And the regress disappears." Thus children at the age of six can know that at four they saw — in the sense of reliably responded to — a fire, although at the age of four all they could do was say 'fire' parrot-fashion, without knowing there was a fire.[16] The important difference is not one of responsive disposition but one of capacity to endorse. The six-year-old has moved into the space of giving and asking for reasons; he can commit himself to a claim and be treated as authoritative; he is responsible for the claim he undertakes. For this he must at least be able to tell what he is thereby committing himself to and what evidence would entitle him to it, that is, he must understand his claim. But even that is not sufficient. For this new normative status is socially conferred. No nonepistemic description of the candidate reporter suffices for the conferral of this status, unless and only insofar as the community conferring that status, treating the individual as responsible, reliable, and so on, takes it to be sufficient. Compare achieving one's majority and being able for the first time to undertake contractual obligations. This status consists in the community's recognition of it. Some minors are more reliable at carrying out the commitments they undertake than many over the age of twenty-one, but this fact does not make their signature mean

---

16. Commenting on this point for the 1963 edition, Sellars said that his thought was that one could have direct (in the sense of noninferential) knowledge of a past fact which one could not conceptualize at the time that it occurred.

that they have entered into a contract. This is how "the light dawns slowly over the whole": at some point one masters the moves, inferential and noninferential, sufficiently that one's noises come to be taken by one's community as having the significance of making claims, undertaking commitments, giving reasons.

*Section 38:* The only sense in which there is no foundation for empirical knowledge is the sense in which the observation reports, which in a certain sense are its foundation, themselves rest (not inferentially, but in the order of *understanding* and sometimes of justification) on other sorts of knowledge. Observation reports, whether of inner episodes or outer happenings, do not constitute an autonomous stratum of the language—a game one could master though one had as yet not mastered the inferential use of any expressions. That is, Sellars rejects *only* claim (2) of the three foundationalist theses considered in [32]. But there is no need for a foundation in this sense: "Empirical knowledge is rational, not because it has a foundation but because it is a self-correcting enterprise which can put any claim in jeopardy, though not all at once."

# Part IX [39]–[44]
## Science and Ordinary Usage

*Sections 39–44:* Here Sellars sketches his Scientific Realism. He includes this discussion because if science is viewed in the opposite, positivist fashion, the notion of inner episodes as theoretical entities, which he is about to introduce, is incoherent. Thus [41] claims that "science is the measure of all things. . . ." This is a view about the authority of claims couched in scientific vocabulary relative to the authority of claims couched in other vocabularies. [43] briefly indicates the positivist view. According to the positivist scheme, there is an observation language in which data are formulated and the results of experiments expressed. All we directly know about are the objects of observation (observation reports are the Konstatierungen of [33]). According to this account, a theoretical language is introduced in order to systematize our observations and facilitate prediction and control. But the objects the theory postulates are virtual, mere calculational devices or instruments for the expression and systematization of observations. Theories are instruments, and their assertions should not be taken as entailing the existence of the objects they postulate. Sellars points out that only someone who thought that the observations themselves were given, not the product of the learning of concepts with which to report, would be tempted by this picture. Once it is discarded, another way of thinking about the distinction between theoretical and observable objects and concepts comes into view.

According to Sellars's view, the distinction between purely theoretical objects and observable objects is *methodological*, rather than *ontological*. That is, theoretical and observable objects are not different kinds of things. They differ only in how we come to know about them. Theoretical objects are ones of which we can only have *inferential* knowledge, whereas observable objects can also be known noninferentially; theoretical concepts are ones we can be entitled to apply only as the conclusions of inferences, whereas concepts of observables also have noninferential uses. But the line between things to which we have only inferential cognitive access and things to which we also have noninferential cognitive access can shift with time, for instance, as new instruments are developed. Thus when first postulated to explain perturbations in the orbit of Neptune, Pluto was a purely theoretical object; the only claims we could make about it were the conclusions of inferences. But the development of more powerful telescopes eventually made it accessible to observation, and so a subject of noninferential reports. Pluto did not undergo an ontological change; all that changed was its relation to us. (Notice that this realism about theoretical entities does not entail scientific realism in the sense that privileges science over other sorts of cognitive activity, although Sellars usually discusses the two sorts of claims together.)

It might be objected to this view that when the issue of the ontological status of theoretical entities is raised, they are not considered merely as objects in principle like any others save that they happen at the moment to be beyond our powers of observation. They are thought of as *unobservable* in a much stronger sense: permanently and in principle inaccessible to observation. But Sellars denies that anything is unobservable in this sense. To be observable is just to be noninferentially reportable. Noninferential reportability requires only that there are circumstances in which reporters can apply the concepts in question (the dimension of inferentially articulated endorsement) by exercising reliable differential dispositions to respond to the objects in question (the causal dimension), and know that they are doing so. In this sense, physicists with the right training can *noninferentially* report the presence of mu mesons in bubble chambers. In this sense of 'observation,' nothing real is in principle beyond the reach of observation. (Indeed, in Sellars's sense, one who mastered reliable differential responsive dispositions noninferentially to apply normative vocabulary would be directly observing normative facts. It is in this sense that we might be said to be able to *hear*, not just the noises someone else makes, but their *words*, and indeed, *what they are saying* — their *meanings*.)

Once one sees that observation is not based on some primitive sort of preconceptual awareness (the tortoise beneath the elephant), the fact that some observation reports are riskier than others and that when challenged we sometimes retreat to safer ones from which the originals can be inferred will not tempt one to think that the original reports were in fact the products of inference from those basic or minimal observations. The physicist, if challenged to back up his report of a mu meson, may indeed justify his claim by citing the distinctively hooked vapor trail in the bubble chamber. This is something else observable, from which the presence of the mu meson can, in the right circumstances, be inferred. But to say that is not to say that the original report was the product of an inference after all. It was the exercise of a reliable differential responsive disposition keyed to a whole chain of reliably covarying events, which includes mu mesons, hooked vapor trails, and retinal images. What makes it a report of mu mesons, and not of hooked vapor trails or retinal images, is the inferential role of the concept the physicist noninferentially applies. (It is a consequence of something's being a mu meson, for instance, that it is *much* smaller than a finger, which does *not* follow from something's being a hooked vapor trail.) If *mu meson* is the concept the physicist applies noninferentially, then if he is sufficiently reliable, when correct, that is what he *sees*. His retreat, when a question is raised, to a report of a hooked vapor trail, whose presence provides good inferential reason for the original, noninferentially elicited claim, is a retreat to a report that is safer in the sense that he is a *more* reliable reporter of hooked vapor trails than of mu mesons, and that it takes less training to be able reliably to report vapor trails of a certain shape, so that is a skill shared more widely. But the fact that an inferential justification can be offered, and that the demand for one may be in order, no more undermines the status of the original report as noninferential (as genuinely an observation) than does the corresponding fact that I may under various circumstances be obliged to back up my report of something as red by invoking my reliability as a reporter of red things in these circumstances—from which, together with my disposition to call it red, the claim originally endorsed noninferentially may be inferred.

## Part X [45]
## Private Episodes: The Problem

*Section 45:* Sellars starts by setting the problem that will occupy him for the rest of the essay: "the problem of how the similarity among the experiences of *seeing that an object over there is red, its looking to one that an object over there is red* (when in point of fact it is *not* red), and *its looking to one as though there were a red object over there* (when in fact there is *nothing* over there at all). Part of this similarity, we saw, consists in the fact that they all involve the . . . proposition . . . that the object over there is red. But over and above this there is, of course, the aspect which many philosophers have attempted to clarify by the notion of *impressions* or *immediate experience.*" Sellars's response to this problem will not be fully in place until [62].

Next Sellars summarizes [32]–[38] (the meat of his epistemological discussion): we now recognize that instead of coming to have a concept of something because we have noticed that sort of thing, to have the ability to notice requires already having the concept, and cannot account for it. For to notice something—to be aware of it in the sense relevant to assessments of sapience, rather than of mere sentience—is to respond to it by applying a concept, making a noninferential judgment about it. So until one has the concept 'green,' one cannot notice or be aware of green things, though one can respond differentially to them—obviously, in ways other than by applying the concept *green*. The title of this essay is "*Empiricism* and the Philosophy of Mind," but Sellars never comes right out and tells us what his attitude toward empiricism is. One might think he endorses it, misled by remarks such as he offers in [6] in discussing the inconsistent triad of commitments characteristic of classical sense-datum theories. For there he dismisses the option of rejecting the third element of the trilemma by doing no more than observing that to abandon it would "do violence to the predominantly nominalistic proclivities of the empiricist tradition" (proclivities that he discusses in more detail in [24]–[28]). But to interpret this remark as an endorsement *by Sellars* of the nominalistic proclivities of empiricism that he invokes here would be to mistake the role the remark plays in his argument. It is often hard to tell when Sellars is speaking in his own voice, and this is one of the occasions on which he is not. It is the classical sense-datum theorists who are committed to this tenet of empiricism, not Sellars—although, as will emerge just below, he does as a matter of fact share with empiricists the belief that "the capacity to have classificatory beliefs of the form '$x$ is $F$' is acquired."

Indeed, we can see at this point that one of the major tasks of the whole essay is to dismantle empiricism. For traditional empiricism depends on episodes of nonverbal, nonconceptual awareness, which serve both as the raw material for a process of abstraction by which concepts can be formed and grasped, and as our warrant for the ground-level (noninferential) applications of those concepts. (Compare [34].) This whole picture depends essentially on the Myth of the Given. Sellars's own view is one he is elsewhere happy to call 'rationalist':[17] conscious experience presupposes that the experiencer already has concepts, and so cannot account for their acquisition. In this claim, Sellars aligns himself with the Leibniz of the *New Essays*, writing against his Lockean target. Sellars's task in the rest of the essay is to show how the philosophy of mind can understand inner episodes once one has rejected *both* Cartesianism *and* empiricism, having recognized that both depend upon the Myth of the Given.

The classical pre-Kantian rationalists, having won their way through to the realization that awareness in the sense that distinguishes us from prerational animals presupposes the possession of concepts, took it that that claim committed them to seeing concepts as *innate* — perhaps not all concepts, but at least the most basic or general ones. Sellars shows that that is not so. For he shows how to put together

a) reliable differential responsive dispositions, causally keyed to things; and

b) inferential uses of concepts, which actually apply to those things,

*each* of which can be acquired separately, to get the capacity for conscious conceptual awareness of things. He shows us

17. For instance, in his important essay "Inference and Meaning," reprinted in *Pure Pragmatics and Possible Worlds*.

how to build out of those ingredients *non*inferentially elicited reports in which the concepts are applied to the things that causally elicit the reports. In this way he can explain how concepts such as *red* and *green* can be acquired, by a route that does not presuppose preconceptual awareness of red and green things (though it does require the preconceptual capacity to discriminate them, and so to learn reliably to respond differentially to them). That allows him to agree with the empiricists (without indulging in their 'nominalist proclivities'—see [24]–[29]) that "the capacity to have classificatory beliefs of the form '*x* is *F*' is acquired," as he puts the point in [6]. In the rest of the essay, he is going to tell a corresponding story about the concepts *thought* and *sense impression*, ending with our capacity to be directly (in the sense of noninferentially) aware of them.

His question at this point is, If this rationalistic 'psychological nominalism'[18] is right (and Sellars insists that it is), how could we come to have the idea of an inner episode? Descartes thought it a satisfactory answer to this question that we get the idea just by having inner episodes. But this must now be rejected as a sufficient condition of our noticing (being aware of, believing that we have) them, for that is just the Myth. The empiricists thought we could get the concept of thoughts and impressions by abstraction from the thoughts and impressions we were already in any case aware of. That too is a version of the Myth. "In short, we are brought face to face with the general problem of understanding how there can be inner episodes—episodes that is, which somehow combine privacy in that each of us has privileged access to his own, with intersubjectivity, in that each of us can, in principle, know about the other's." In other words, how

---

18. Here 'nominalism' has a sense quite distinct from that invoked in the previous paragraph, picking up on its use in [6]. See [29].

could we ever have come to know that reports of the form 'I'm seeing something that looks red,' or 'I am thinking that Vienna is in Austria,' were reliable signs of certain inner facts, given that we can make no empirical correlation by induction as we can with 'This is red'? The Jones myth is the answer to this question—indeed, the only answer available once we have given up both the self-authenticating nonverbal episode notion of Descartes and the empiricists, and the anti-inner-episode strain in Ryle and Wittgenstein (as promised in [10]).

Sellars will "use a myth to kill a myth" [63]. He will tell a story about how a community that turns out always already to have had thoughts and sense impressions might work its way up to having the concepts *thought* and *sense impression*, and then come to be able to apply them noninferentially and so for the first time to notice and be aware of those thoughts and sense impressions. This is explicitly put forward as a myth. Sellars is not claiming that things actually happened this way, that we really had Rylean ancestors, or owe our concepts to a primitive genius (never mind one called 'Jones'). Sellars's pragmatism dictates that issues of conceptual priority be translated into questions of the relative autonomy of different strata of language—that is, into questions concerning what language games can be played independently of and antecedently to which others. Telling an as-if historical, developmental story is a way of exhibiting those relations of conceptual dependency and presupposition.

## Part XI [46]–[47]
## Thoughts: The Classical View

*Section 46:* The previous section explained (contra Ryle) that there really are impressions to be accounted for. This section just says the same thing about thoughts. There isn't much in the way of argument here: Sellars points out that it is hard to explain these things away, and we may agree that a theory that can keep them is, other things being equal, superior to one that must deny them.

*Section 47:* This bit is directly addressed to Ryle, and dismisses his claims that

a) 'privileged access' must mean invariable access — which Sellars rejects because often someone else can tell what I must have been thinking, even when I am not aware of having thought it; and

b) introspectible thoughts are just *sotto voce* verbal imagery: words running through one's head, 'perceived' as if the words were either heard or seen. (This point is discussed further in [56].)

We have to free ourselves from these preconceptions if we are to understand Sellars's positive story about thoughts and sense impressions.

## Part XII [48]-[50]
## Our Rylean Ancestors

*Section 48:* Sellars introduces the notion of 'our Rylean ancestors,' who have and can talk about dispositional traits that are relatively long term, the sort of thing for which Ryle's account works well: beliefs, desires, hopes, fears, plans, moods, character traits, etc. Ryle got these more or less right (we'd still have to put holist qualifications on his atomistic approach), but he injudiciously thought that his success at giving dispositional-behavioral accounts of this sort of mental phenomenon meant that anything that could not be explained this way must be metaphysical and illegitimate. Sellars, via Jones, will show that this is not so. Sellars insists (on the basis of the distinction between dispositions and episodes) that having subjunctive conditionals of the Rylean sort does not yet give the Ryleans the ability to talk about thoughts and experiences. Sellars is going to show what additional conceptual resources they need to develop the concept of *thoughts*, and then on that basis, the concept of *sense impressions*.

*Section 49:* The problem is, what would have to be added to the Rylean language so that those who speak it "might come to recognize each other and themselves as animals that think, observe, and have feelings and sensations as we use the terms." (The last clause is meant to eliminate the merely dispositionally analyzable bits of mentalistic discourse — items, paradigmatically such propositional attitudes as beliefs and desires, that are psychological, but do not qualify as mental *episodes*.) The first requirement is *semantic* discourse (see [30]). Semantic discourse falls on the side of the epistemic. It is not "definitional shorthand for statements about the causes and effects of verbal performances," although it may have such statements as contingent consequences. Semantic discourse is a kind of *normative* discourse, discussing how expressions *ought* to be used, or are *properly* or *correctly* used. This is one of Sellars's most fundamental ideas, appearing in nearly all of his earliest essays. ([51] and [52] will tell us about the second requirement.)

*Section 50:* "My immediate problem is to see if I can reconcile the classical idea of thoughts as inner episodes which are neither overt behavior nor verbal imagery and which are

properly referred to in terms of the vocabulary of intentionality, with the idea that the categories of intentionality are,
at bottom, semantical categories pertaining to overt verbal
performances." This latter idea is that thought must be understood by analogy to talk, in the sense that the concepts
we put in play to talk about the meanings or contents of our
thoughts are understood in terms of their role in their original
or 'home' language game of talking about what we *say*, rather
than about what we *think*. (Compare Dummett's commitment
to understanding judging as the interiorization of an act of
asserting, rather than understanding asserting as the exteri-
orization of an act of judging.)[19]

## Part XIII [51]–[52]
## Theories and Models

*Section 51:* Here Sellars returns to the discussion of theoretical
language (discussed under the heading "Scientific Realism"
in Part IX). Theoretical discourse is just a sophistication of
a dimension of ordinary empirical language. One way it can
arise is by model and commentary. Sellars is telling us this
because "the distinction between theoretical and observational discourse is involved in the logic of concepts pertaining
to inner episodes."

*Section 52:* So "the second stage in the enrichment of their
Rylean language is the addition of theoretical discourse."
This matters because Sellars claims that "the distinction between theoretical and observational discourse is involved in
the logic of concepts pertaining to inner episodes."

19. Michael Dummett, *Frege's Philosophy of Logic* (New York: Harper and Row,
1973), p. 362.

## Part XIV [53]–[55]
## Methodological versus Philosophical Behaviorism

*Section 53:* Jones is a forerunner of methodological behaviorism (which is clarified below, and which Sellars endorses).

*Section 54:* Behaviorists need not present their accounts as
analyses of the concepts we already employ; nor need they
introduce their theoretical notions by means of explicit definitions. The former would be analytic or logical behaviorism,
the latter a kind of instrumentalism. Both are mistakes. Instead, the behavioristic requirement that all concepts should
be introduced in terms of a basic vocabulary pertaining
to overt behavior is compatible with the idea that some behavioristic concepts are to be introduced as *theoretical* concepts, relative to a behavioral observational vocabulary. This
view becomes available once one sees (as we did in [39]–
[44]) that the distinction between theoretical and observable
objects is methodological, not ontological, i.e., that it has to
do with our access to those objects, either purely inferential
or also noninferential, and says nothing about the kind of
object involved. To say that they are theoretical concepts in
this sense is to say that (at this stage in the development of
the language game) they can only be applied as the conclusions of inferences. Thus they are not equivalent to any
descriptions of behavior (which could be applied observa-
tionally). This idea is one of Sellars's cardinal innovations.

*Section 55:* Behaviorism in this methodological sense is compatible with physicalism, since the theoretical concepts it
employs might turn out to refer to neurophysiologically de-

scribable items (just as 'Pluto,' introduced as a name for whatever is perturbing the orbit of Neptune, might have turned out to apply to an astronomical ball of cheese). But it is also compatible with denying such physicalism. Behaviorism and physicalism are two different and independent sorts of commitment.

## Part XV [56]–[59]
## The Logic of Private Episodes: Thoughts

*Section 56:* Jones's model for thinking is inner speech. His commentary ensures that this is not conceived of as verbal imagery. What is objectionable about the verbal imagery proposal (introduced in [47]) is that it consists in the use of a quasi-perceptual model: hearing the wagging of an inner tongue.

*Section 57:* The model carries the applicability of semantical categories over from overt utterances to thoughts; so thoughts can be 'about' things.

*Section 58:*

(1) This Jonesian theory is compatible with dualism as well as with materialism.

(2) Inner episodes are to be unobservable the way molecules or the cause of the crack in the dam are, not the way ghosts are. That is, we happen (at this stage in the story) not to be able to report them non-inferentially, though there is nothing that rules out such observation in principle. Thus they might turn out to be identical to physiological events. Neverthe-

less, at this point only the third-person use is available, even for characterizing our own episodes.

(3) One can't think until one has learned to speak — one can't assert anything 'mentally' (think to oneself that . . .) until one has caught on to the social practice of public assertion. Thus talk is prior to thought in the order of explanation. Once one has learned simultaneously to talk and think, however, thought often precedes talk in the order of causation.

(4) So the notion of language having a meaning, being 'about' things, is not to be explained in terms of thoughts having meanings (for instance, in the Cartesian or Lockean fashion). The project must explain the meaning of thoughts in terms of the meaning of talk, which must be explained some other way (e.g., in terms of social practices).[20]

(5) Jones does not think of these episodes as immediate experiences, that is, things to which thinkers have privileged access, since he doesn't have this concept yet. His episodes are 'inner' only in the mundane sense of 'under the skin.'

*Section 59:* But it turns out that when Jones teaches his theory to other people, they "can be trained to give reasonably reliable self-descriptions, using the language of the theory, without having to observe [their own] overt behavior." That is, one can develop a conditioned reflex in someone (perhaps depending on some ultimately discoverable neurophysiological event related to his thought) to report noninferentially what heretofore could only be inferred. "What began as a

20. "Intentionality and the Mental" (a symposium by correspondence with Roderick Chisholm), *Minnesota Studies in the Philosophy of Science,* pp. 507–539.

language with a purely theoretical use has gained a reporting role." It might not have turned out this way. But insofar as Jones's theory is a good one (a question in principle independent of the eventual identifiability of these episodes with ones characterizable in neurophysiological terms), his fellows were *already* reliably differentially responding to these episodes. So one would expect that they would be able to learn to expand their differential responses to include reports. This story explains why: recognizing "that these concepts have a reporting use in which one is not drawing inferences from behavioral evidence, [the account] nevertheless insists that the fact that overt behavior is evidence for these episodes is built into the very logic of these concepts, just as the fact that the observable behavior of gases is evidence for molecular episodes is built into the very logic of molecule talk."

## Part XVI [60]–[63]
## The Logic of Private Episodes: Impressions

*Section 60:* Jones now does for sense impressions what he previously did for thoughts. This category presupposes the category of thoughts. We start from a sub-class of thoughts called 'perceptions.' Seeing that something is the case is an inner episode in the Jonesian theory, which has as its model reporting on looking that something is the case. But these perceptions are not yet sense impressions. We still have a kind of *claim*, something in the epistemic order, not a kind of *particular*, something in the causal order. To get sense impressions we need the notion of a 'state of the perceiver' common to those occasions when the perceiver is right and those occasions when he's wrong about there being something red and triangular. This will be the 'intrinsic characterization' of impressions that Sellars talks about in the third paragraph of [45], and in [22]. Here is an outline of the theory of perception on the causal side that was appealed to in [7].

*Section 61:* Whereas thoughts were modeled on sentences, impressions are modeled on pictures or, more generally, replicas, which are particulars. The essential feature of the model is that visual impressions stand to one another in a system of ways of resembling and differing that is structurally similar to the ways in which the colors and shapes of visible objects resemble and differ. That is, there are states of the perceiver which, though neither red nor triangular, have features (call them 'of-red' and 'of-triangular') that are isomorphic to the kinds of features visible physical objects have. This is a sort of functionalism about sense impressions. The occurrence of these replicas is to be understood as a nonepistemic relation of particulars (which neurophysiology or dualistic mind science might further specify for us). "Thus the model for an impression of a red triangle is a red and triangular replica, not a *seeing* of a red and triangular replica," which would be an epistemic affair. Their overall explanatory role can be summarized thus: It is sense impressions "which (from the standpoint of the theory) are being responded to by the organism when it looks to the *person* as though there were a red and triangular physical object over there."

*Section 62:* This section just does for sense impressions what [59] did for thoughts. It points out that people can be trained to develop conditioned reflexes for reporting these theoretical entities called 'impressions.' (Perhaps some neurophysiological mechanism will be discovered eventually that explains the acquisition of such responsive dispositions.) At this point, since Jones's students can make noninferential reports of their sense impressions as well as of their thoughts, they are directly (in the sense of noninferentially—the only sense available once the Myth of the Given has been rejected) aware of both sorts of inner episode. In the case of sense impressions, this is awareness of the impressions "of the sort which is common to those experiences in which we either see that something is red and triangular, or something merely looks red and triangular, or there merely looks to be a red and triangular object over there" [45]. Such noninferential reports of sense impressions, reports of the form "I am now sensing a sense impression of a red triangle," are quite different from those made using 'looks,' which were considered in the first half of the essay. A noninferential report using 'looks' takes a 'that' clause as its content-specification, and indicates the inferential potential that is being forwarded as a candidate for endorsement. A noninferential report of a sense impression takes a description of a particular of a sort modeled on replicas as its content-specification, and indicates the causal antecedent common to reports of how things are and of how things look. (Recall the diagnosis of [7].) Running the two together would re-enact the Myth of the Given. These two essentially derivative and parasitic strata of language, both centering on noninferential uses, express different aspects of perceptual experience. The conceptual awareness of sense impressions that Sellars has now made available in an unmysterious and unthreatening way is the "something more" that (according to the opening sentences of [16]) our perception involves, besides endorsement of propositional contents "wrung [noninferentially] from the perceiver by the object perceived." They are what was promised in the first paragraph of [45]. The sense impressions of which we are aware (once both the concept of sense impressions and the corresponding noninferential reporting practices are fully in place) *explain* the fact that "when I say '*X* looks green to me now' . . . my experience is, so to speak, intrinsically, *as an experience* indistinguishable from a veridical one of seeing that *x* is green [16]." For both sorts of speech act arise as the result of exercising reliable differential dispositions to respond to the presence of sense impressions — as they did already before Jones gave us the concepts without which we could not be aware of them. All that needed to be added to those responsive dispositions was the new concept *sense impression,* with the kind of inferential articulation appropriate to its model of *replicas* of, e.g., visible surfaces.

Sellars has now completed his task. We now have recipes telling us how to diagnose and treat the Myth of the Given in all its multifarious manifestations, whether what is given shows up in the guise of particulars whose occurrence entails knowing or believing something (e.g., sense-datum theories), or in the form of noninferentially acquired propositionally contentful beliefs (e.g., what is expressed by 'looks' talk). Epistemologically foundationalist appeals to the given of the Cartesian sort have been shown to fail because *non*inferential uses of concepts (no matter whether their subject matter is construed as 'inner' or 'outer') turn out to presuppose *inferential* uses of concepts. Empiricist appeals to the preconceptual given to explain concept acquisition (whether by abstraction or otherwise) fail because "we now recognize that instead of coming to have a concept of something because we have noticed that sort of thing, to have the ability to notice a sort of thing is already to have the concept of that sort of thing, and cannot account for it" [45]. Nonetheless, Sellars has shown us how we can make sense of the idea that

we have direct awareness of mental episodes (the applications of inferentially articulated *concepts* of thoughts and sense
impressions elicited noninferentially *by* thoughts and sense
impressions), including the limited but very real privileged
access each of us has to such inner episodes, without committing ourselves to the Myth of the Given.